ALSO BY ANOOP CHANDOLA

Folk Drumming in the Himalayas: A Linguistic Approach to Music

Situation to Sentence

AN EVOLUTIONARY METHOD
FOR DESCRIPTIVE LINGUISTICS

by

ANOOP CHANDOLA

Foreword
by
Robert Austerlitz

AMS PRESS

NEW YORK

Library of Congress Cataloging in Publication Data

Chandola, Anoop.
    Situation to sentence.

    Bibliography: p.
    1. Linguistics—Methodology.   I. Title.
P126.C48   410' .1'8   78-07125
ISBN 0-404-16038-7

MANUFACTURED IN THE UNITED STATES OF AMERICA

CONTENTS

FOREWORD

There was a time when linguistics lived within its modest means and pursued its modest aims. These had originally been defined by the outside world. Somewhere on the road to the present day, because of metabolic changes induced by aging, morphology dried up and dropped out of grammar, thus permitting phonology and syntax to swell up and take up the slack. Drunk with its early successes, syntax became bloated and intruded on the preserve of meaning-in-general which, in revenge, challenged the very foundations on which syntax had been built in the first place. The challenge and the ensuing strife affected practitioners in various ways. Some of the older ones were demoralized or alienated. The younger ones, growing up in such a bustling environment, chanted slogans and lived beyond their means, pursuing remote aims situated in the outside world. The New Linguistics had learned how to pose and how to answer ambitious, abstract questions because it was a Theory and not a Method.

This book starts from modest beginnings, lives within austere, self-imposed means, and pursues aims meticulously described by the outside world. It is an attempt at answering some of the original and simple questions for which the New Linguistics was too powerful. It grapples with a method which, incidentally, gives the nudge to a number of ambitious claims. See how it works.

Robert Austerlitz
Columbia University

PREFACE

In the present work the reader will several times see the statement that current linguistic approaches fail to explain the natural organization and interaction of various linguistic units in the development of a sentence. I have, however, directed my main criticism toward the transformational-generative (TG) approach, the most widely accepted phrase-oriented theory of structuralism. It was developed more than two decades ago, when there was no regular working approach available for syntactic analysis, except the crude method known as immediate constituent or IC analysis. Very soon, like its predecessor the IC method, the TG method too began to display its own serious drawbacks.

Scholars tried and are still trying to do patch-up work on the TG model. But patch-up work does not help much when the underlying fundamental principles are not sound. The analyst unfortunately is forced to work within the limits of an established approach, even when he knows it cannot solve the real problems. This is what happened with me when I had to complete a transformational dissertation in the Linguistics Department of the University of Chicago in 1966 in order to receive my Ph.D. degree (see bibliography). James D. McCawley agreed with me that there were no answers for some of the problems I wanted to discuss in my dissertation; I was, and am, most appreciative of his frank opinion. However, in 1966, after receiving my Ph.D. degree, I immediately started the search for a more powerful approach. The result, as presented in this book, is a radically different theory and method of language description, with some implications for historical linguistics.

In the search for causal explanations, several drastic departures became inevitable. These departures have been emphasized over and over again in this work. There are, however, some minor but relevant aspects which have not received adequate emphasis in this book. A few comments on them, therefore, will not be out of place here.

Like the myth of 'phrase', many other notions have gained popularity in linguistics. One is the view that there exist structural spaces or slots which are filled by certain symbols or units. Consider a rule like:

$$Z \rightarrow A/W - Y$$

—or "Z is rewritten as the A that occupies the space between W and Y" so that the string is WAY. We cannot explain the evolution of eyes by saying that there are two holes on the human face which are filled by two eyeballs, resulting in the organs called 'eyes'. Artificial bodies may be made this way, but natural ones do not grow in this manner. This is reminiscent of our old elementary school instruction system, in which language drills were patterned very much like the above 'fill-in-the-blank' type rule. Since this is certainly not the way a child learns his native tongue, we have thus abandoned this style of rule writing.

We have contended in the following chapters that rules must be evaluated, not just on logical grounds, but also on historical, psychological, and pragmatic grounds. In this respect we have shown several weaknesses of the TG rules. One of them is that TG rules involve inefficiency which the brain would not allow. This refers to the "waste" produced by the useless repetition and redundancies of symbols in the TG rule system. It may appear logical to justify these redundancies on the ground that language, as a noise channel, does involve a certain amount of redundancy in order to prevent loss of information in actual communication. We must note, however, that total communication of situations involves not only verbal but also several other non-verbal systems. Scholars working in such fields as semiotics (Morris 1946, etc.), kinesics (Birdwhistell 1970), ethology (e.g., Smith 1977), not to mention several other social and behavioral disciplines, have clearly shown the significance of non-verbal systems in the transmission and reception of messages. In the total context, communicative redundancies may not be considered redundant if they provide some sort of additional information or serve some other function. Contextless analysis of unilinearly transcribed speech texts or sentence types cannot account for total information. It is necessary to employ sound movie audio-visual texts, such as those used by psychotherapists, for better information analysis (cf. Scheflen 1973). Our main concern in this book is to deal with the role of grammatical system in externalizing a situation that has been internalized by a speaker. The redundancies of symbols that we find in the T rules (transformational rules) have no correlation with grammatical system or total communication. In fact, as will be shown in this book, the T rules, like the rules of other phrase-oriented grammars, distort information that is indispensable for explaining, not only the descriptive, but also the historical development of sentences.

It should not be concluded that the descriptive method of English given here was developed with the history of the English language in mind. In fact, the present work is based on my earlier draft, "Experience and Expression—An Evolutionary Theory and Method in Language Description." The paper prepared on the basis of this draft in 1973 was published in 1975 (see Bibliography). I started examining the theory and method proposed here in historical terms after I had already submitted this paper for publication in 1973. In 1976, I presented a paper entitled "Historical Evidence in an Evolutionary Description" at the Second International Conference of Historical Linguistics at the University of Arizona, Tucson.

However, the entire work as presented here is the outgrowth and result of ten years of labor. The ideas expressed in this book owe much to the influence and stimulation of works by such scholars as Pāṇini, Bhartṛhari, Mammaṭa, Ferdinand de Saussure, Sapir, Bloomfield, Firth, Martinet, Pike, Chomsky, and many, many others who are not mentioned in the following chapters. This book is based also, as mentioned above, on my previous draft and on papers on which many scholars have commented. All these comments have been very encouraging. I am especially grateful for the comments of the following scholars: Raimo Anttila, Henning Andersen, Dwight Bolinger, Thomas Sebeok, Paul Turner, Cecil Rogers, Jr., William Christie, Jr., Stephen Tyler, and William Shultz. I am especially indebted to Robert Austerlitz for his inspiring words. While teaching a course on the present theory and method, I employed some of my American students as native informants of English. Among them I am most thankful to Kathleen Moore, who not only worked on the manuscript as a native speaker of English, but also typed it. My debt to my wife Sudha cannot be adequately expressed. Any mistakes that the reader may find in this book are soley due to my oversight or ignorance.

Speaking of mistakes, one may wonder why I have not used the conventional system of abbreviation. I would like to comment on this minor departure here, although it has no relation to the theory and method presented in this book. English spelling is so inconsistent that it considerably impairs the basic learning skills of school children in the two Rs. One wonders what could be the consistent principle that abbreviates 'reading', 'writing' and 'arithmetic' as the three 'rs'. Those who argue for the pronunciation of the first sound say that it is 'rithmetic' for 'arithmetic'. Let us confess openly that linguists have been ineffective in improving the English spelling system. But at least we can improve its abbreviation system in our own discipline. I have made an attempt here to abbreviate terms in a consistent manner which would allow more predictability of the full form. Appendix A explains our principle of abbreviations and lists all of them with their full forms. Readers accustomed to old abbreviations, which are not always uniform in all approaches anyway, will find in this book every rule followed by its explanation, including the full form of every abbreviation.

Finally, I urge all those who are involved with language study in any way to examine new linguistic ideas very seriously before they decide to break away from the traditional notions we have shown to be false. Language descriptions have time and again given the false impression that sentences are formed through some hierarchy of structural divisions, constituent grouping, phrases, transforms, etc. This has made current linguistics very difficult to penetrate where it is most needed, such as at the pre-college level. It is as difficult to justify the use of such false notions as it is to justify current English spellings. We use both such traditional linguistic notions and spellings because we are used to them. We spell the word *through* or *tough* or *thought* with letters which do not represent their phonetic reality in a consistent manner. Similarly we spell a sentence as subject and predicate, or NP plus VP, or SOV, SVO, VSO, and even OV, etc. (where N = Noun, P = Phrase, V = Verb, S = Subject, O = Object). Yet we do not have a shred of evidence to prove that humans (or non-humans) really base their situations first in such bipartite or tripartite constituents or phrases. The inner linguistic reality of the human brain has not been clarified by the descriptions of language based on the linear oral production of sentences. How can we undo the "brainwashing" of centuries if we do not keep our minds open?

I
NATURALISTIC THEORY

In linguistics a great deal of emphasis has been placed on a formal approach, but it is not always clear what is formal and what is not. In a literal sense, a formal approach is needed only when there are forms to be dealt with. A formal linguistic theory, then, deals with linguistic forms, whatever they may be. One basic goal of any scientific theory should be to deal with the nature of these forms; thus the most central aspect of a formal theory should be to learn how a particular form comes about in the first place. If a theory either cannot explain or ignores those causes or conditions that are directly responsible for the evolution of forms, then it has weakened its claim to being called a formal theory, no matter what other practical advantages it may have. Evolution ordinarily implies that some entity or entities grow or change in a given environment, in a sort of action-reaction or cause-and-effect chain. Language entities are also constantly growing. Thus, whether one talks about the historical development of linguistic entities through different stages of time, or about how a speaker assembles those entities at a given time, the process is still evolution. In other words, whether we deal with diachronic or synchronic formation, the point is still the same: evolution.

The term evolution is more commonly used to refer to the growth of a natural body. For instance, consider a human body. What one sees as a human body or its constituent structural parts are the result of many entities that grew into successively larger and larger entities or units. For example, there are various chemicals plus rules which form genes; genes are grouped into chromosomes by certain rules. In this manner cells, tissues, and other larger or higher units are formed. Each unit affects the other lower or higher units according to rules. Thus by the action-reaction chain, or cause-and-effect relationship of various units, the ultimate product is a natural form, which we call the human body.

If the goal of a linguistic theory is to understand the natural development of a form, then it should possess a method that would reveal such information or knowledge in terms of rules. There may not be any end to such information, but the goal is to reveal at least that information which is most relevant in the evolution of a form. Before the advent of transformational-generative methodology, abbreviated here as TG, we found an attempt to reach this goal, however indirectly. But in the TG approach many new and interesting issues were brought up; linguists paid considerable attention to these new issues, so much so that the fundamental goals were sidetracked. The result is that even today linguistic methods fail to describe the formation of natural linguistic units, e.g., concepts, words, sentences, etc., in a way that will mirror their actual evolutionary track in a synchronic or diachronic sense.

The following examples will illustrate what has been said here and in the preceding paragraph. One might hear these Hindi-Urdu words: *dūd* 'milk', *dudhārū* 'milch', *dūdhiyā* 'milky', *bāg* 'tiger', *bāghin* 'tigress', *bāghaũ* 'tigers', etc. We see here that in some word-positions there is a voiced dental stop *d,* whereas in other word-positions we see its counterpart, a voiced aspirated *dh.* Similarly, *g* and *gh* alteration takes place. The history of Hindi-Urdu is well recorded from its Old Indo-Aryan stage right down to the present day. Nonetheless, irrespective of historical documentation, we can give the following rules to cover the sound change seen in these Hindi-Urdu examples.
1. *dh, gh* #→ *d, g* #
which reads that *dh* and *gh* are replaced by *d* and *g* respectively in word-final position. When we have more data we can generalize even more to determine that 'an aspirated sound occuring word-finally is replaced by its corresponding unaspirated sound.' What this formulation means is that *dūd* would be represented basically as *dūdh.* Similarly, the base of *bāg* would be represented as *bāgh.* The aspiration of the base form is preserved in non-final positions, like *dūdhiyā* 'milky' and *bāghin* 'tigress', but lost in the final position, e.g., *dūd* and *bāg.*

The assumption that *bāgh* is the base form is made purely on descriptive grounds. That is, Rule 1 describes a synchronic change in the simplest way, according to our data. This rule, however, points to the actual historical development. If we go through the Sanskritic and Prakritic stages, representing respectively Old Indo-Aryan and Middle Indo-Aryan, we find that Sanskrit has *dugdha* and Prakrit *duddha,* corresponding to the Hindi base form *dūdh.* In actual Devanagri writing, the Hindi forms appear with aspiration as *dūdh, bāgh,* etc. This demonstrates that Rule 1 correctly indicates the direction of evolution, not only synchronically, but also diachronically. Thus Rule 1 yields far more information than is apparently needed for limited descriptive purposes, hence it is a very powerful rule. Such rules become especially necessary where we do not have any comparative or historical evidence and must resort to internal reconstruction of forms. Grassmann's Law had already demonstrated the need for such formulations. Another aspect of Rule 1 is that it states clearly those conditions or causes by which *dh* and *gh* are replaced by *d* and *g* respectively; this rule would be useless if it did not state that such a change takes place word-finally.

But Rule 1 describes only one kind of evolution. There are other aspects to be considered too, if we think of several smaller entities growing into a larger one. For example, we need rules to describe the formation of the word *bāghin* 'tigress'. From the data given above it is easy to figure out that *bāgh* is the basic concept, while *in* is a modifier concept. That is, *in* is selected by the speaker to modify the concept *bāgh* in order to refer to the 'female of the tiger'. We need to have rules that will indicate that *bāgh* and *in* exist before the formation of *bāghin.* The speaker actually follows this direction or track when he assembles or composes concepts into a larger forma-tion. The oblique plural suffix for nouns, as seen in *bāghaũ* 'tigers', represented by *aũ* (pronounced ɔ̃), can also be selected for *bāghin;* placed after *in* it will thus yield *bāghinaũ* 'tigresses'.

Here we observe that the speaker selects concepts out of a given list and linearizes them in a sequence. Selection and linearity together are the two operations which we call 'grammar'. The speaker can select *aũ* only after *bāgh* and *in* are selected. He can position *aũ* only after *in* has been placed after *bāgh.* What we mean here is that the speaker does so because his intention or goal is to form the word *bāghinaũ* 'tigresses'.

The larger composition *bāghinaũ* is possible only when there are smaller units like *bāgh, in* and *aũ.* The speaker will change *bāgh* to *bāg* only if he finds that *gh* is the last sound of the word. This means that Rule 1 can apply only after all the intended concepts which are represented by abstract sound units have been selected and placed in proper order to form a complete word. In other words, rules likewise must follow an order. This order mirrors the evolution; if it does not, it is then not a natural order.

The kind of reasoning as shown in the development of Rule 1 is implicit in the works of Bloomfield (1933) and others who followed him, especially in the description of morphemes and their sounds. For convenience we can call it evolutionary reasoning. This reasoning can be taken further, along the lines found in Pāṇini's description of Sanskrit in his Aṣṭādhyāyī. For example, *bāghin* has another plural *bāghinẽ,* besides *bāghinaũ.* The plural suffix *ẽ* is added to the feminine nouns ending in a consonant. However, this is only one condition; before this condition we should know whether *bāghin* selects primary ending, or secondary ending, and so on. The feminine suffix *ẽ* represents primary ending in the plural, whereas the suffix *aũ* represents secondary ending in the plural for all nouns. Before we can learn about the selection of the type of endings, we have to know what case is represented by a particular ending type. That is, the formational rules first take care of case, then of ending type, then of the actual suffix representation of the ending, and finally of rules like Rule 1. Actually there will be many other rules, such as the stem formation rules, prior to the selection of an ending type. Thus, there is a gradual chain of formation, always developing higher forms from lower ones with a cause-and-effect relationship. In other words, before a word, and finally a sentence, is formed, various kinds of information are fed in, and accordingly various rules apply in an order that represents the actual evolution from smaller elements to larger ones.

If rules are required to provide formational information on linguistic units, then we find current syntactic descriptions failing to meet this requirement. Consider, for instance, a few syntactic rules of the so-called base component in the TG approach, as developed by Chomsky (1957, 1965):

2. S → NP + VP or S → NP + Aux + VP
3. VP → V + NP
4. NP → (Art) N (S)
where S = Sentence, N = Noun, V = Verb, P = Phrase, Art = Article.

If there are any reasons for S being developed into or replaced by NP + VP, etc., the rules in the base component do not reveal them. Rule 2 does not explain how the NP is selected nor how it occurs first and the VP next. Should it be assumed that the NP is placed there because it is implicitly the subject, or is to to be interpreted as subject because it occurs in that position? The two operations of selection and linearity are confused in rules like 2–4. Logically selection and linearity cannot take place simultaneously. One might, however, argue that for convenience of quick reading and economy it is necessary to imply selection and linearity simultaneously. The counterargument is that scientific rules explain how certain things happen under certain conditions; when those conditions are present, those specific results will take place with those particular things. In order to reveal such a process or development, the number of symbols and rules and the format of those rules are immaterial. Science is more interested in insightful statements than in readable or economic ones. And the fact is that a grammar with rules based on a natural cause-and-effect principle will eventually yield far greater economy and simplicity, due to more generality. But this fact can be realized only after quite a large amount of data has been described.

When we speak of cause-and-effect we want to know whether in Rule 2 the symbol S causes the generation of NP + VP. If S is developed into NP and VP, then the implication is that S exists prior to the formation of NP and VP, just as the implication in Rule 1 was that *gh* exists prior to *g* in those Hindi-Urdu examples. It is erroneous to assume that a human body exists before its genes, chromosomes, cells, tissues, etc. However, rules like 2–4 are decompositional in their format. The division of a structure S into NP + VP or NP + Aux + VP is as arbitrary as dividing a human body into broad constituents like 'Head + Bust + Bottom' or 'Head + Bust + Hands + Stomach + Legs', etc. Such an arbitrary division may be useful for some purposes, but it comes nowhere near to approaching the actual evolution of that human body. If we consider a sentence to be a natural body, then we cannot start its formation with its largest components. To cut a sentence into constituents like 'phrases' is a completely artificial method, which was initially influenced by the principle of 'immediate constituents' or the IC approach. (See for instance Wells 1947.) The IC approach in turn was influenced by the old habit of imagining a sentence to be Subject and Predicate. If the ICmethod and phrase structure rules fail to mirror the formation of sentences in the natural sense, then the base component rules of TG also fail in this goal, since the base component is likewise based on the notion of phrase.

The grouping of various stems or words and even sentences into phrases is arbitrary and poses serious problems. The phrases of Rules 2–4 can be given for almost any language in some order. Consider, for example, Rules 2 and 3 as two base rules for Hindi. It would mean that in Hindi the first noun phrase or NP_1 is selected for the subject function and is placed before VP. But the fact is that NP_1 can be placed not only after V, but also after the second noun phrase, or NP_2, which implies the function of object. NP_1 can also occur right between NP_2 and V. That is, we have at least these four possibilities: (i) $NP_1 + NP_2 + V$; (ii) $NP_2 + NP_1 + V$; (iii) $V + NP_1 + NP_2$; (iv) $NP_2 + V + NP_1$. If one were to hear Hindi sentences, he would have difficulty in considering one of these possibilities as the base rule. Suppose we accept (ii) or (iii) as the base, then grouping NP_2 as a constituent of VP, as characterized by Rule 3, is impossible. The TG advocate, therefore, would have to see whether it could be justified that NP_2 is within VP. This is possible if (i) or (iv) are picked as the base rule. Nonetheless, we still have to resort to arbitrariness to select (i) or (iv) as the base. Such an arbitrariness becomes unnecessary if we do not insist on the TG principle that one of the structures of (i)–(iv) is base and the rest are its transformations or derived from the base.

Suppose we accept the order $NP_1 + NP_2 + V$ as the base, simply because this one is more frequent than all others, even though frequency has not been considered as the valid reason in this connection. But aside from frequency we have no clear reason for accepting (i) as the base structure. Now transform (i) into (ii) as: (i) $NP_1 + NP_2 + V \rightarrow NP_2 + NP_1 + V$. The TG analyst would now be convinced that NP_2 is still part of VP. There would be a problem, however, if a language has only the orders $NP_2 + NP_1 + V$ or $V + NP_1 + NP_2$. Hindi, of course, does not pose such a problem, since it has other orders besides these two. A more subtle problem, however, arises when we want to present our description as the most efficient one. The most valid criterion of efficiency is that there is neither duplication nor repetition of symbols or rule operation. Suppose the mind or brain should operate with efficiency. Then TG formulations imply that in order to generate (ii) the brain first employs (i) as the base. What it means is that the brain first uses the symbols NP_1, NP_2, and V as in (i), and then repeats them in (ii) as NP_2, NP_1, and V, except that the two NPs have exchanged their positions. These are simple examples of the inefficiency of TG rules, which of course may be eliminated within the TG framework, but only in a few cases. Otherwise, the notion of transformation is bound to be inefficient by repeating wholly or partially the same symbols on both sides of the arrow. (See Appendix B for TG problems with unordered phrases.)

The other question is this: Is not the order or sequence of symbols in the base structures, or their transforms, the reaction of some smaller elements that have already taken place much before such base or deep structures? In the Hindi examples we see the word endings or inflections represented by *ẽ* or *au* in the noun words *bāghinẽ, bāghau,* and *bāghinau.* The pronouns, verbs, and adjectives are also marked by endings. It is a well-known fact that because of these word endings the word order becomes very flexible. Suppose *bāghinẽ* is NP_1 and NP_2 is *bāghau,* then they can be recognized as such in any orders of (i)–(iv) given above. In a language like English, where there are very few overt word endings, the word order appears much more rigid when compared to that of Hindi.

It becomes then obligatory that rules of word formation must apply before the rules of word order. It also leads us back to the point that in natural growth smaller elements form larger elements in a chain of cause-and-effect. If we miss this chain somewhere, then we cannot explain the affected formations. Missing this chain leads to duplication or redundancy of operations. Below we want to give an example of this.

One major function of inflections or endings is to express the relations between, for example, subject, object, verb, etc. That is, such words can be complete only when the endings have been selected and placed properly. Selection of endings is possible only when such relations are previously known. But Rules 2–4 imply that such relations (subject, object, etc.) are positionally or linearly defined. For instance, suppose that NP_1 is implicitly subject, and therefore placed before VP. That is, the position of NP_1 in Rule 2 serves the function of subject. Then later, by other rules, proper endings will be attached to this NP. The questions are these: What is the need for ending later if the function of subject is already defined by its position in Rule 2? Why does the brain have to resort to two kinds of operations—linearity of phrases and then inflectional affixes— to express one and the same function? Such a redundancy of operations should not exist in an efficient system. This suggests that the order and hierarchy of rules and components is not natural in TG or other approaches.

This discussion, even though simple and brief, clearly warrants the need for a natural formal approach that will reveal the order or track through which linguistic forms are actually developed or evolved. This order must indicate that mental processes produce sentences with optimum efficiency. In the following chapters, an evolutionary compositional theory and method of language description is presented, with the aim of searching for such a natural order. The naturalness of the description ultimately can be evaluated in terms of rules like Rule 1, which enable us to see beyond the present of a given language. How our evolutionary approach does so can be understood in chapters five and six. In other chapters we will see how inadequate the phrase oriented approaches, such as TG, are in solving problems of a far more serious nature.

The biggest inadequacy of such structural theories lies in the fact that they do not consider the pre-existence of a 'situation'; in reality the speaker *uses* symbols only to express that 'situation'. Why the lexically determined meaning (the literal or basic meaning) of symbols can be reversed or modified, without a change in the so-called structure, cannot be adequately understood or explained without the notion of 'situation'. The evolutionary theory to be proposed in the following chapters will demonstrate that the *use* of concepts and functions depends on 'situations'. It will show why a sentence can be structurally perfect and yet schizophrenic, indicating mental confusion, and hence not really well-formed.

In short, a theory whose goal is to explain the evolution or formation of a given sentence must be pragmatic in some sense. The situational view to be initiated in the next chapter, and expanded in later ones, is motivated by several such pragmatic considerations.

II

SITUATIONAL VIEW

Let us imagine a situation A which has a particular 'boy', one 'girl', some 'sweet fruits', and an activity 'giving', which the boy does every day. The speaker views these items not in any sequence or linear order, but rather as a network of relationships. Thus to him the boy has the relationship of 'giver' (or 'actor' of the activity 'giving'); fruits are the object of the activity 'giving'; the girl is the recipient of that object and the time period of that activity is located in terms of 'day'. If the speaker speaks English, the sentences might eventually turn out as:

(1) *The boy gives sweet fruits to a girl every day.*
   or
(2) *The boy gives a girl sweet fruits every day.*

Incidently, a sentence or any part of it italicized in this book implies that its representation is in broad, abstract, phonetic symbols or sounds, not in orthographic letters. For example, *the* must be understood as $\eth\partial$ in the sense of 'definite article'.

We have to assume that the speaker has a system of selecting and linearizing these items in a particular order. This system is called grammar. Linearization is motivated by the phonetic material; because of neuro-physiological constraints, man's vocal tract produces only one sound at a time. Even our earliest human ancestors must have experienced situations like the one underlying (1) and (2), but they could not manipulate their vocal tracts the way their descendants could later. Even today we can observe that those adults who cannot speak (such as those deaf by birth) can understand the items and their relationships in a situation like that of (1), unless mentally retarded in some way. We can see this with animals too, especially farm animals. These animals can understand simple factual case relationships like 'giver', 'object', 'recipient', etc., in situations of an activity like giving. Animals can react to various situations as needed; they would simply fail to react if they did not form at least some sort of primitive analysis of a given situation.

Here by the term analysis we mean that a situation is perceived in terms of items which are considered different from each other by the viewer or speaker. This is a very important point which is to be emphasized: The situation a person experiences is analyzed. Otherwise we could not talk of the relationship existing among the items of a situation. Man may or may not speak out his experienced items of a given situation, but they still exist. Linearization is required only when vocalization of the situation items is needed. This all suggests that a non-linear state of experienced items exists even before the human's vocalization of them. That is, the selection of items and their relations already exists before their linearity. Hence, selection and linearity are two different stages of evolution, and the rules must thus reflect them as two separate operations, applied in the order of selection first and linearity second. This necessitates the convention that a linearity rule will always apply to a unit only after some selection rule or rules have been applied, no matter where such rules occur in the grammar.

Let us go back to the situation underlying (1) and (2) in order to better explain selection and linearity operations. The speaker has observed in his own way some functional relationship among the items of his situation. For instance, 'boy' is experienced by the speaker as the actor or subject, 'fruit' as the object, 'give' as the activity or verb, 'girl' as the recipient, and 'day' as the time locative. Thus we have these cases for the verb 'give': subject, object, recipient, and time locative. There may be other cases, but in this situation the speaker observes only these. A case is a direct participant in an activity. The items 'sweet', 'every', 'the', and 'a' are also participants in the activity 'give', but only via the items they specify. For example, 'boy' is a direct participant as the actor or subject of the activity 'give', while 'the' is a specifier for 'boy', meaning some definite boy. This is why it is stated that specifiers or adjectives agree with the items they specify.

After assigning functions to the items of his situation, the speaker feeds the information to the grammar. With the selection operation of grammar the speaker finds the proper lexical concepts to match the items and their functions. The list of concepts can be called a lexicon. Descriptively the concepts are preformed. Historically they are also the outcome of an experience in a situation. Once a concept is produced or formed it can be reused. We actually use a concept in the synchronic sense, but reuse it in a diachronic sense. There are two types of concepts—basic and modificational. The concepts *boy,* *give, girl, day, every, fruit, sweet, the,* and *a* are basic. Suffixes, like the one represented by *s* with *fruit,* the one with *give,* or *to,* are modificational. Some concepts may be basic as well as modificational. A lexical concept has a set of semantic components followed by phonetic components. The speaker picks up *boy,* for example, to match the item 'boy'. The concept *boy* has the semantic features or components 'human, male, young, noun, etc.', and is followed by the abstract phonetic symbols *b,ɔ,* and *y.* This kind of phonetic representation is indicated by italicizing or underscoring the written or orthographic representation of the English example. Thus, *boy* stands for *bɔy.* The speaker continues selecting all the required corresponding concepts and then linearizes them. For example, if he selects *girl, a,* and *to,* he then linearizes them as *to a girl.* The reasoning behind this is that if an item is experienced as an actor for an activity in a statement, then the selected *actor* and the *activity* are linearized as *actor* first and *activity* next. Such a causal development must be explicit in the actual formulation. A grammar which identifies *boy* as an actor or subject merely because it is placed before the activity *give* is not naturalistic, since it fails to indicate the actual direction of events. In a natural grammar it will be clear that *boy* is placed before *give* only after the former has been selected as the actor and the latter as an activity. Incidentally, due to the interaction of selection and linear rules there may be changes in the phonetic representaton of the concepts. These changes too are accounted for by rules implying a cause-and-effect relationship.

The entire formation process of words and the sentence can be represented by the following figure (Figure 1):

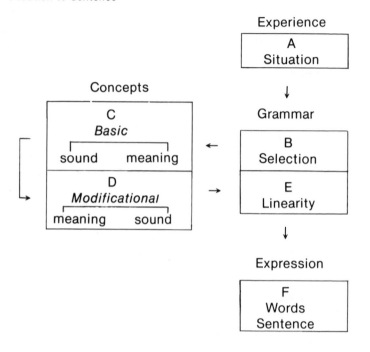

Figure 1

The arrows point out the evolutionary process preceding from Box A to Box F. This process is repeated every time a word or sentence is formed. The Box F stage is followed by actual pronunciation rules. Thus, for example, the sound symbol *b* is described in phonetic terms as 'bilabial voiced stop', giving an instruction to 'articulate *b* by moving this or that part in this or that manner in the vocal tract'.

The implication here is that the base of a sentence is neither in so-called phrase structure or PS rules, such as Rules 2-4 of the preceding chapter, nor in any semantic rules, such as have been suggested by generative semanticists or independent semanticists   like Chafe (1970). The sentence must have its source in a given situation experienced by the speaker. We define the relationships that can exist among the items, such as activity, cases, specifiers, etc., and these relationships are formulated to yield optimum generalization, as will be seen more clearly in the next chapter.

The evolutionary notion suggested in the preceding figure (from Boxes A-F), including the phonation (pronunciation) that follows F, is very important from a psychological standpoint. This figure implies that the psychological process converts the situational items into concepts with the functions as assigned in Box A. This means two things: The entire formation takes place grammatically and unidirectionally. In fact, unidirectionality is a mere aspect of grammaticality.

There is one very vital psycholinguistic issue here which cannot be understood at the present level of research. The issue is that of the order of priority, if at all there is such an order. The above figure indicates that once the speaker decides to pick up concepts, he then has to evolve them into complete words. The question is this: Which basic concept does he, or rather his grammar, start working with while proceding from Box A to Box F? For example, would the speaker's rules start work with the concept *fruit* first and then *boy*, etc.? Or would his grammar first pick up every basic concept in any order and then associate them with the other concepts in any order? Or can his mind leave one concept, which is only half associated with some second concept, behind and, in the meantime, start working on some third concept required for the sentence, and then come back to the original, unfinished, half associated concepts? The mind or brain or nervous system does it so fast, and motivates the articulatory mechanism to produce the entire sentence so quickly, that the whole issue of priority order becomes very difficult to understand. Perhaps this issue can best be illustrated by the following analogy.

Suppose an artist wants to draw a picture of the situation in which a boy gives sweet fruits to a girl. There is no order amongst the items of the situation. Rather the artist has to start working with this or that item. He can first start drawing either the boy or the girl. Or he might decide to draw the legs of the girl first and then start drawing the fruit. Maybe he draws just one fruit for the time being and starts drawing the head of the boy, then returns to finish the figure of the girl or add more fruits to the picture. But think of the artist instead as the human mind which has to speak out the situation instantly. We can see the artist building up the various elements of the picture, but we cannot see the inner workings of the speaker's mind. The only thing we can say for sure is whatever word is spoken first has been completed first at the level of Box F. Which concepts received priority before reaching Box F is not accurately observable. Can we say with assurance that whichever case word or verb word was spoken first was also perceived first?

Thus we face the problem of the ordering of mental decisions taken by the speaker, which are reflected in his grammatical selection and linearity rules. It is possible that if we knew the history of such mental decisions, the ordering of certain rules in this book might have to be changed. Whatever may be the state of future knowledge, it is certain that a word's formation has to pass from Box A through to Box F. It is probable that the speaker might stop a formation (f_1) at the level of Box E, and then decide to pick up another item and start its corresponding formation (f_2), which he might take to the level of Box D. However, the speaker would have to return to Box E and take f_1 to Box F to complete its process. This processing factor seems to be one of the reasons why a speaker in actual performance does not speak a very long sentence with only one tense marker. Hypothetically we may think of words upon words combined to form a giant sentence with only one finite verb, but this does not happen in normal discourse.

Starting points in a sentence might give some clue about priorities in certain and limited cases. Studies by some scholars, e.g., Piaget (1952), Firbas (1966), Coleman (1965), Clark (1965), Prentice (1966), Johnson-Laird (1968), Osgood (1971), Piaget and Inhelder (1971), Carpenter and Just (1972), Sokolov (1972), Kintsch (1974), Lindsley (1975), MacWhiney (1977), etc., seem to be of interest along these lines. But the basic problem of knowing each and every formation which passes through the various psychological processes still remains unresolved. Our major problem, as rightly emphasized by Chafe (1970, 1971), is the direction of sentence evolution.

What we want to emphasize here is that a word formation, and eventually a sentence formation, must complete the route suggested by Boxes A-F of Figure 1, no matter what the order of the priorities suggested above may be. That is, the application order of rules must follow the broad direction of A-F. The following chapters attempt to demonstrate very clearly why and how this goal is achieved.

III

GRAMMATICAL PRODUCTIVITY

Sentences (1) and (2) as given in the preceding chapter are grammatical—grammatical primarily in the sense that they express the situation as it was experienced by the speaker. The speaker decides what to express and it is the speaker who sees the relationship between the items of a situation. The speaker is literally a 'see-er' in this respect. Figuratively, he is a 'seer' who can fabricate things, or who can see items in his imagination in relationships that may be incredible to his listener. Grammar is not concerned with whether or not the listener believes the speaker's experience; the only thing grammar has to do is to carry the situation, as shown in Figure 1, from Box A to Box F. Whatever is given in Box A is not in the control of grammar. Grammar cannot make decisions for the speaker. Box A's contents are the speaker's decision alone. Here lies the main difference between a prescriptive and a descriptive grammar. A grammar which selects certain concepts, only because of other concepts, turns out to be prescriptive, while the grammar that selects concepts because of the situation is descriptive. Grammatical systems in other theories so far have yielded only more or less prescriptive rules, forcing us to look for a truly descriptive grammar. The importance of this departure is illustrated below.

We, in other words, want to know why (1) and (2) are grammatical. The answer is very simple: The speaker felt that 'boy' is the 'actor', 'fruit' the 'direct aim', 'girl' the 'recipient', 'give' the 'activity', and so on. With the selectional operation of grammar the speaker selects from the given lexicon *boy* as the 'subject' case, *fruit* as the 'object' case, *girl* as the 'dative' case, *give* as the 'verb', and so on. The situational relations like 'actor', 'direction', etc., are respectively renamed in the grammar as 'subject' case, 'object' case, etc. The concept *boy,* for example, cannot be selected as a 'subject' until the speaker instructs the grammar that he has assigned 'boy' the function of 'actor' for 'give', which he considers to be the activity. But if the grammar were to select 'girl' as the subject instead of 'boy', the sentence would be:

(3) *A girl gives (sweet fruits to a boy every day).*

If the speaker said *girl* as subject, with the assumption that he was saying *boy,* then the sentence, like (3) above, would be an example of mental confusion. Mental confusion here means that the expression has no correlation with experience; that is, unlike (1) or (2), the situation is not correctly represented by (3).

The evolution of (3) is not from the situation underlying (1) or (2). To assume that (3) is representing (1) or (2) is erroneous and, hence, the selection of *girl* in place of *boy* as the subject case is ungrammatical. This is a new dimension of ungrammaticality. In other approaches sentences (3) would be considered as grammatical as (1) or (2), since in other theories the underlying belief is that words are selected by words, or concepts are selected by concepts, according to their syntactic-semantic features and their mutual compatibility. But on the contrary, in our evolutionary approach concepts or words can be selected only when a situation is present. By not assuming the presence of a 'situation' we might make unnecessary criticisms, such as Lehman (1974) did about the TG notion of NP (as is in our Rule 2). He thinks that subjects are not essential for every language and cites several languages, including some Indo-European languages, as being of the OV (object-verb) type. The following sentence in the Sanskrit of the Ṛgveda is given as example of lack of NP as subject:

(4) agnímīle puróhitam (Ṛgveda 1.1)
 Agni-(I)-praise priest
 '(I) laud Agni the priest'

Here the subject *aham* 'I' is implied by the first person singular ending in the verb *īle.* According to Lehman this sentence is an example of where NP is not needed. However, we can cite other Vedic examples where the pronominal subject does appear, e.g.:

(5) ahám dadhāmi draviṇam havíṣmate suprāvyè yájamānāya
 sunvaté (Ṛgveda 10:125)
 I   hold   wealth. . . .
 'I hold wealth. . . .'

where *aham̐* 'I' is the subject of the verb *dadhāmi*. Thus, even in Vedic hymns pronouns are overtly given as subjects. The point, however, is not whether the subjects are pronouns, or whether the verb is active or passive, pseudopassive, reflexive, or medio-passive. The proper question to ask is what the language would do if it had a situation such as that underlying (1) or (2). Even a language like Sanskrit, which Lehman labels as OV (object-verb) type, has to have an overt subject like *bālakaḥ* 'boy' for (1). The Sanskrit equivalent of (1) or (2) would be:

    (6) pratidinam dadāti bālikāyai madhurāṇi phalāni bālakaḥ
        every-day gives to-girl   sweet   fruits boy
      'Every day (the) boy gives sweet fruits to (a) girl.'

The placement of linear position of the subject, object, verb, etc., would be more or less free in (6), but that does not make any difference as far as the need for the subject *bālakaḥ* 'boy' (nom. sg.) is concerned. The point is that the grammar of any and every language will have to produce the subject 'boy' if its presence is felt in the situation.

An overt pronominal subject is not needed in (4), because the first person verb can imply *aham̐* 'I'. Also, the octosyllabic meter of (4) cannot admit more syllables. *Aham̐* 'I' would have added two more syllables, thus violating the phonetic pattern of the meter. This metrical problem does not arise in (5) where we do have *aham̐* 'I'. In other words, the true causes of having the subject manifested or not are not those of Lehman. An automatic by-product of this is the conclusion that such typological classifications as SOV or OV are not merely redundant, but lack the penetrating insight of linguistic evolution as well. If we were to tell a non-linguist that English is an SVO (subject-verb-object) language, he or she might chuckle and ask, "Want to bet on that? Let's toss a coin. Heads I win; tails you lose." And thus we lose the argument over SVO.

We have shown here that *girl* cannot be admitted as the subject in place of *boy* if the underlying situation is (1) or (2). But another aspect of grammaticality became very important in the TG approach, and subsequently influenced other approaches, such as that developed by Chafe (1970). Chomsky and Chafe, for example, would consider (3) to be grammatical, while feeling sentences such as the following to be either deviant or

possessing a low degree of grammaticalness:
   (7) *The sweet fruits give a girl to the boy every day.*
   (8) *Golf plays John.*
   (9) *The chair laughed.*

In their approaches there would be constraints on selecting *golf* as the subject of *play*. They assume that there would be rules in existence which would not allow the speaker to say (8) or (9). Such a view seems to resemble that of Whorf, in which the basic assumption was that the speaker's thinking is influenced by linguistic structures. One might even advocate the exaggerated view that man speaks because there are linguistic structures. Nevertheless, the evolutionary fact is that the so-called linguistic structures are there because man speaks or communicates. That the idea of selectional constraints as suggested by Chomsky or Chafe is theoretically unnecessary can be demonstrated practically by the following test. We might ask why the speaker did not say *woman* in place of *boy* in (1) or (2). The answer would be that it was a 'boy', not a 'woman', whom the speaker considered as the actor of the activity 'give'. If he had considered it a 'woman', then the sentence would have been:

   (10) *The woman gives sweet fruits to a girl every day.*

Similarly, if the speaker thinks that it is 'John' who does the activity of 'play', then why would he replace John by 'golf'? He would replace 'John' with 'golf' only if he felt that it was 'golf' which was doing the activity of 'play'. There is no method which can predict the thinking of a speaker. Suppose for the time being we devise a rule that 'golf' cannot be the subject of 'play', since 'golf' does not have the semantic feature 'animate'. But then how could we stop *golf* from becoming the subject of *play* in the following sentences:

   (11) *How can golf play John?*
   (12) *John can play golf, but golf cannot play John.*
   (13) *Perhaps in your country golf can play John, but not in my country.*
   (14) *Golf will play John if golf becomes animate.*

Our argument is simply that the speaker will make 'golf' the subject if he thinks or imagines 'golf' to be the actor of 'play' in his particular situation. The fundamental question is not whether the speaker can say (8) or not; descriptive grammar is concerned rather with the question of how rules can ultimately express what the speaker intended in terms of his real or imaginary experience. Grammatical validity does not lie in proving whether a situation is false or true. The sentence *Three and three makes four* is as grammatical as *Three and three makes six,* if neither of these sentences presumably distorts the situational understanding of the speaker. There is no need of selectional constraints, or some kind of sub-categorization rules, to take care of a sentence like *Her husband is pregnant.* I have heard all sorts of arguments in regard to such sentences. One, for example, is that you will be able to say this sentence some day when science makes it possible for an adult male human to become pregnant. As listeners we do not need to wait for such a scientific miracle. A listener might hear this sentence and wonder what happened to her 'husband'. But the listener is wondering over the abnormality of the message or information, not at the well-formedness of the sentence. This astonishment is due to unfamiliar information, which is not sufficient, however, to declare a sentence ungrammatical; the sentence perfectly carried the message the speaker wanted it to. While the sentence *Delhi is the capital of America* is considered to be well-formed, who would wait to see the possibility of truth in the sentence's information? This is the power or strength of language, in that it is capable of expressing not only so-called normal thinking, but also so-called abnormal or wishful thinking. It has been one of the most unfortunate implications of TG that what is natural, and what is the strength of language, has been labeled as its weakness and curtailed by such impossible means as selectional constraints. Language is only a tool with which to reveal what the speaker knows or thinks of his situation. Linguistics, if it is to be a science, must give up its role as an ethical or moralistic discipline, making judgments on the experience of the speaker. Descriptive grammar does not deal with the question of what can or cannot be said. It rather devises rules to account for whatever is said.

Thus grammar is relieved of the impossible and unnecessary task of devising rules for selectional restrictions. Humans are imaginative beings and no one can fathom a speaker's potential for visualization, since it is unlimited. What we can do is to describe those limited relations through which the speaker can see those unlimited combinations of items or concepts. Those of us who have taught not only language and linguistics, but literature know very well how suggestive (8) and (9) could be in certain contexts and hence be quite grammatical.

The issue of selectional constraints is actually not new. Several Indic linguistic philosophers (sixth to ninth centuries A.D.) discussed *yogyatā* 'compatibility' as one of the three essential relations that exist among the constituent concepts of a sentence. (The other two are *ākāṅkṣā* 'expectancy' and *saṁnidhi* 'contiguity'.) The notion of *yogyatā* means precisely such selectional constraints as suggested in TG. For instance, a Sanskrit sentence like *agninā siñcati* '(He/she/it) wets (it) with fire' is illogical, since it fails to meet the requirement of *yogyatā*. (see Raja 1963 for more details.) This failure is considered to be due to the fact that 'fire' does not possess that property or potential or feature that could do the action of wetting. Grammarians in practice, however, considered the whole issue of *yogyatā* or selectional constraints useless. Indic literary theories (which are deeply influenced by linguistic thought) resolved the issue by assigning three types of meaning to a word. These meanings were named after their underlying powers which are *abhidhā* 'literality', *lakṣaṇā* 'metaphor', and *vyañjanā* 'suggestivity'. Thus any word is capable of having three meanings, namely literal, metaphorical (figurative), and suggested meaning. All of these meanings can be expressed simultaneously or one at a time. Thus, what may not be accepted at the literal level of meaning would be acceptable at the figurative or suggested levels of meaning. Literary theories are far more realistic than present day linguistic theories at observing actual language behavior. (For further discussion see Raja 1963.)

Here is an example of a literal and metaphorical meaning for one and the same concept: The concept *tiger* has roughly the literal semantic components or features 'Animal, Male, Cat family member, Noun, Tiger, etc.'. Since it is one of the strongest animals, a quality of strength and bravery is also associated with this concept; thus this quality or feature can be made the focus for metaphorical meaning. That is, a literal feature can be made the focus whenever needed. If there is a brave man named 'John' in Chicago, then the speaker might feel the same way toward John as toward the tiger and say:

(15) *John is a tiger.*

The statement in (15) is not false. What the speaker has done is to emphasize the metaphorical meaning, so that 'John' is not to be considered as having the other semantic components, like 'Animal of the cat family, with tail, paws, furry skin, etc.'. There may be another man named 'Ray' who is a coward. With this situation in mind the speaker may say:

(16) *Ray is a tiger.*

And the listeners will laugh, because the focus is now on the opposite of the strength or bravery that a tiger exemplifies. Thus here we see another progression, or the development of one figurative meaning into another figurative meaning. The 'tiger' now changes from 'brave' in (15) to 'coward' in (16). The laughter can be explained only on this basis of evolution: 'tiger' → 'brave' → 'coward'. The listener indirectly confirms this cause-and-effect chain by laughing, on the basis of his actual knowledge of the situation, e.g., that Ray is really a coward. It would be totally unpsychological if one tried to derive syntactically this metaphoric sentence as *Ray is not a tiger* → *Ray is a tiger*. Why would the human mind go through the entire syntactic formation, repeating all the symbols on both sides of the arrow, and delete the negative symbol *not?* Instead, we need simply to make a general convention that:

5. Opy Focus meaning → Opposite Meaning

This rule states that whatever may be considered as the focus of meaning feature can be replaced by its opposite meaning. The symbol 'Opy' stands for 'optionally', which means that this rule applies optionally. This rule is an optimum generalization and it indicates how the speaker can exercise his imagination to the fullest possible extent. Humans do have reasons to use their imagination, whether or not a grammarian understands such reasons. Grammarians need only to make rules to reflect how humans convert this imagination into language. Unfortunately to the contrary, the TG grammarians have sought to control the natural faculty of imagination by imposing artificial selectional constraints. We gain nothing by such attempts to control, unless our purpose is not language description, but something else, e.g., behavior control.

Above we gave a case of optimum generalization in order to show how rules map creative verbal behavior. Every speaker has the potential of creating new concepts and when new concepts are created there is also the possibility of new sound sequences. Speakers can improvise with the existing semantic and phonetic material to make new sequences. For example, an English speaker may say *English people can pronounce sp, but not zp at the beginning of a word.* (Here we are implying that *sp* and *zp* are pronounced as [sp] and [zp] respectively.) Now normally in English grammars and dictionaries there would not be any mention of the concepts or words *sp* and *zp* of this sentence. However, the moment this sentence was said by an English speaker it forced us to accept *sp* and *zp* as real concepts and words of English, no matter that linguists have declared that there is no possibility of any such words with an initial sound sequence like *zp.*

Let us illustrate this point further. Suppose we give a rule that English can have potentially a sound sequence *bir,* but not *sbir.* That is, *sbir* would be ungrammatical in English. The list of lexical entries would then include *bir* whenever it becomes really part of English lexicon. In reality, however, it is impossible to know which concepts have already taken place with what sound sequences. At least in this book *bir* and *sbir* have already become part of the English lexicon; they have been used in this paragraph. No one would ever be able to list all the concepts and their sound sequences used by all the speakers of the English language. This is a universal phenomenon, which means that to explain grammar by means of semantic or syntactic description of every lexical entry is impossible. For practical purposes, however, we assume that there is a list of concepts without end. That is, descriptively an individual speaker does have a list in his head. What we need is a grammar rule that would produce endless concepts with endless combinations of sounds. Here is just such a rule:

6. Bae

6.1 Come Stem

where Bae = base, Come Stem = complete stem.

These two rules can be interpreted as only one rule; the rule with the decimal point is part of the whole number rule. What 6 and 6.1 mean is that a base is defined as a complete stem (Come Stem). The term 'complete stem' indicates that the stem has reached its complete form, in terms of semantic and phonetic units in the given situation. In other words, the speaker associates with the concept all those features which finally make it a word in a sentence. Thus if the situation calls for plurality of the items 'sp' and 'zp' the plural would be *sps* and *zps*. Here the bases would be *sp* and *zp* from the concepts *sp* and *zp* respectively.

There are many other serious reasons why this rule is needed and there are exceptions which have to be stated. All reasons and exceptions will be discussed in the fifth chapter. For the present suffice it to say that without rules like 6–6.1 we could not account for the unlimited capacity for producing new concepts with regular or irregular sound sequences. This then makes our position different from that of linguists like Halle (1962), whose phonological rules would admit a new concept only with regular sound sequences, like *bir* but not *sbir* or *zp*. We, of course, do not have generative phonology type rules for the sound sequences within a concept, because we assume that a concept has the sounds and their order inherent in it. For example, we do not have to specifically state that English has the word initial sound sequence *st-*, but not *sd-*. The reason for not doing so is that we will not list any concept in the lexicon with an *sd-* sequence. On the other hand, there will presumably be concepts listed in our lexicon such as *state, step,* etc., which will automatically imply the existence of the *st-* sequence, thus eliminating the need for any separate rule about *st-* type clusters. Thus, the inclusion of any specific phonological rules allowing *st-*, but not *sd-*, would be redundant. However, if some speaker should instantaneously make a new concept with *sd-*, Rules 6–6.1 would already account for it. (See Rules 70–71).

Rule redundancy and repetition of symbols are eliminated by optimum generalization. It appears that the human mind or brain operates with optimum generalizations, while simultaneously taking care of all particulars, with a minimum of waste. While it is difficult to prove the existence of such mental operations, it still remains valid to state that an efficient description ought to have a limited number of rules which regulate virtually unlimited data. We want to demonstrate that such regulation is possible only in terms of the cause-and-effect chain.

Consider the 'dative case'. A case rule maps the situational experience of the activity, and the items directly related to its performance, onto the selection of concepts. Thus dative case can be defined as:

7. Date

7.1 Ret ÷ Acy

where Date = dative, Ret = recipient, Acy = activity. The division sign '÷' means 'of'. Rule 7 is defined by Rule 7.1 It means a dative item is that party which is the intended recipient of the activity or verb. In (1) or (2) 'girl' is the dative, since it is felt by the speaker as the ultimate item receiving the activity 'give'. That is, in the situation of 'giving' the activity of 'give' is aimed at 'girl'. Note that a recipient is a non-actor party, whereas a receiver is an actor (subject), e.g., *he* is 'receiver' (actor) in *He receives fruits.* As shown below more rules follow:

8. *to* : Date

which reads '*to* occurs with the dative (Date) case item'. The colon sign ':' means 'occurs with' and represents a selectional rule only, never a linear rule. Also, this sign is unidirectional, which means that *to* occurs with Date, not that Date occurs with *to*. Rule 8 selects *to* for the dative word, but since it is a selectional rule, not a linear rule, it does not state where to place the *to*. So we add linear rules. The plus sign ' + ' means 'Place now' in such rules.

9. + Prepon

10. + Adje

11. + Cae

These three rules define that place: i.e., the preposition word is first, then the adjective word, and finally the case word, which yields the sequence *to a girl.* There may be exceptions to the general rule. Such exceptions will be given after the general rule, with the convention or ordering that, when there is conflict, the rule which comes later (or is with the higher numeral) is more powerful than the earlier one, i.e., the rule with lower numeral, unless otherwise stated. This is why numbering of rules is very relevant. These details will be given in the successive chapters. But for the moment consider the generality produced by Rules 7 and 7.1. These two rules actually make only one rule when the decimal point is counted as part of the whole number. However, in a detailed grammatical description there may be more than one such part with separate conditions or exceptions attached, in which case it is necessary to refer to each of the decimal point parts of one whole number, as was done in 7 and 7.1 One must not, therefore, confuse the economy of rules with generalization, when the basic purpose is to achieve the optimum generality plus the inclusion of all the exceptions. The numbers given to the rules have the primary function of ordering the evolutionary steps through which forms are produced. If we were to cut away the so-called superficial numbering of rules, we could have written Rules 9–11 as one rule in the form (Rule 12) shown below:

12. Prepon + Adje + Cae

But we would still have three symbols, namely Prepon, Adje, and Cae, and so we would really have gained nothing by rewriting Rules 9–11 as Rule 12. Besides, the rule format seen in Rules 9–11 has the advantage of integrating as many symbols in a continuity with minimum repetition. This can be further observed in the word order rules given in the following two chapters. More will be seen later concerning this aspect of economy. But for now we want to demonstrate how Rules 7 and 7.1 together achieve tremendous economy via generality. Consider the following sentences:

(17) (i) *The boy slips sweet fruits to a girl...*
  (ii) *The boy passes sweet fruits to a girl...*
  (iii) *The boy moves sweet fruits to a girl...*
  (iv) *The boy delivers sweet fruits to a girl...*
  (v) *The boy sends sweet fruits to a girl...*
  (vi) *The boy brings sweet fruits to a girl...*
  (vii) *The boy carries sweet fruits to a girl...*
  (viii) *The boy takes sweet fruits to a girl...*
  (ix) *The boy flies sweet fruits to a girl...*
  (x) *The boy sings to a girl...*
  (xi) *The boy praises him to a girl...*
  (xii) *The boy tells a story to a girl...*
  (xiii) *The boy gets the fruits to a girl...*
  (xiv) *The boy goes to a girl...*

    (xv) *The boy walks to a girl...*
    (xvi) *The boy runs to a girl...*

And we could continue adding on many other verbs which have a recipient item. Whenever the speaker experiences this item plus other co-occuring items in an activity, he selects a matching verb concept from his lexical list. In all the sentences of (17) the activity implied by a verb is being received by another item. Rules 7 and 7.1 designate an item like 'girl' as dative case, being the recipient of an activity (verb); any exceptions to this rule can be taken care of in a detailed description by adding more rules. In other linguistic methods, such as TG, there would be all sorts of lexical, syntactic, and semantic classifications of verbs and nouns, such as Vb_1 *to* NP_w, VB_2 *to* NP_w, VB_3 *to* NP_w, etc., which only make the list longer. Listing should be resorted to only when there is no alternative. Rules of the 7–7.1 type are the alternative. This alternative explains why all verbs Vb_1, Vb_2, Vb_3, etc., take 'girl'; it pinpoints the cause of all these different verbs behaving alike in a given situation. The economy is self-evident when Rules 8–11 apply to yield the sequence *to a girl.*

    The sequence *to a girl* is evolved without arbitrary notions of breaking word sequences into some kind of constituent called 'phrase'. Compare, for example, Rules 2–4, where *to a girl* would be included first as part of VP, then of NP, and so on. We have mentioned earlier examples of the articles *a* and *the*. Articles are adjectives, not only in the descriptive sense, but also in a historical sense; this fact, however, is not revealed by TG rules. For instance, Rule 4 makes articles basic constituents of an NP, whereas *sweet* would become part of the phrase *the sweet fruits* only after a T rule application. That is, in a phrase there is no set boundary for different members of one and the same major class. Consider, too, the tagmemic approach of Pike (1967), where *to a girl* would appear as a 'filler' phrase of the slot 'Indirect Object' at the level of clause. In other words, different approaches have different presentations of phrase constituents. This difference is actually due to the fact that phrase has no formal reality, unlike a word or sentence. And the question of the formal reality of a phrase does not arise because it has no psychological reality. Above, we have shown that what is described often in terms of phrase, can just as easily be described without it. In successive chapters, it will be further demonstrated why there is no need of phrase anywhere. Any unit whose psychological and formal evolution cannot be determined in certain terms must be judged ungrammatical.

Case rules like 7 and 7.1 deal with the functional relations of situational items. Case rules link concepts only in the context of such relations. The notion of case is not new; Pāṇini (c. 400 B.C.) has rules similar to those proposed here. But the notion of case developed by Fillmore differs from the one we are proposing. His notion is within the framework of the generative approach and faces almost all the problems which TG has. My criticism of TG, therefore, applies to Fillmore's approach also. One should, however, not label our approach as a new case theory; I, like many others, was taught Hindi-Urdu (one of my mother tongues) and Sanskrit with the notion of case always present, right from the seventh grade on. Besides case relations, there are other relations which link the situation to a grammar. The notion of specifiers such as adjectives, adverbs, etc., are necessary to link the situational items with the concepts. For example, the item 'sweet' specifies 'fruit'. This specification of 'fruit' is also decided by the speaker at the situational stage of (1).

This chapter demonstrates that grammar rules must produce a sentence according to the speaker's decisions for every item in the given situation. If, for example, the speaker feels that *girl* is the recipient of *fruits,* then Rules 7–11 will eventually ly produce the sequence *to a girl* as seen in (1). On the other hand, if the speaker decides to see *fruits* as the recipient of *girl* in a situation, then Rules 7–11 will produce the sequence *to sweet fruits,* yielding a sentence like *A boy gives a girl to sweet fruits.* This sequence and this sentence are grammatical because that is the way the speaker saw or viewed the items of the situation of this particular sentence. The purpose of language is to express what the speaker views in a situation, not what the actual situation is. There will be no end of our description if we believe that language should express the reality of the items in a situation, irrespective of the view of the speaker towards those items. Items and situations are endless; we do not understand, and as linguists it is not even within our limits to understand, the real purpose of every item in every situation. Since these endless items and situations can be viewed by the speaker only in terms of a limited set of general functions or relations, it is possible to produce a sentence. These are the relationships that a grammar can describe. A grammar is productive if it evolves sentences according to the view of the speaker. Rules which attempt to control the view of the speaker are restrictive or prescriptive, not descriptive. The efficiency of descriptive rules lies in the fact that they do not distort the information which the speaker intends to convey, even though this information may be true or false on various other grounds. The power of language is such that it can communicate not only true information, but false as well. The truth of the linguistic universe is not the same as that of the extra-linguistic one. The source of linguistic truth is the situational view of the speaker. That is, the speaker analyzes a situation according to his or her understanding. It is this analysis which the brain converts accordingly into a sentence. The sentence is true to this analysis, not necessarily to the factual status of the situation. A speaker's understanding may or may not vary from that of other speakers. This explains why it is possible to have different analyses of one and the same factual situation. Sentence is a means of presenting the situational analysis of the speaker to the hearer.

In this chapter we saw how 'selection' has been misunderstood in connection with grammatical production of words and sentences. The following chapter demonstrates how the role of 'linearity' has been misunderstood in the subtle explanation of sentence formation.

IV

LINEAR PHASE

To the listener, the singlemost important means for comprehending the message is linearity. However, it is true that linearity came much later in human evolution. Linearization is not any continuous line, but rather a chain made up of dots of successive sounds; because normally one sound alone can be articulated at a time, concepts too have to be linearized. So linearity also works for the speaker who wants to take the message to the listener. And the listener decodes the message, starting right from the beginning with the speaker's first word. But there are some basic differences between the linearity and the selection of concepts. One can observe how difficult it is to create or institute a new regular sound in decades or even centuries, yet how easy it is to create a new concept. How easy it is to combine some noun-concept with another noun-concept, but how difficult it is to change the position of a suffix or prefix! There are virtually unlimited basic concepts in a living language, but the sounds and positions for these concepts are strictly limited. Whatever is limited can be controlled by means of rules; sounds and positions could have been altogether unlimited, but to what purpose? The purpose of communication would not have been served if a language has thousands of sounds and linear positions. The nature of language is such that it employs a finite system to convey the potentially infinite experience of speakers to their listeners.

Such nature is revealed by the grammar rules of linearity. Linear rules are devised in such a way that we can place *girl, to* or *to girl a.* Rules 9-11 precisely yield this. Likewise, we can produce only *gives,* but never *sgive,* in the sense of the verb *give* with third person singular 'present' in English. If the functional relations of items on the one hand, and of linear positions on the other, were not limited, then there would be no possibility of communication and hence no question of grammar. Linear positions are related to the functions of items, but only after the set of concepts in a given situation has been selected. This relationship existing between itemic functions and linear positions is not always simple to describe. Two decades ago TG described this relationship in an over-simplified style; this became quite a topic for discussion at the time, especially in connection with structural ambiguities, an example of which is given below:

Chomsky thought that TG has more explanatory power because it could resolve ambiguous constructions like that in (18):

(18) *The killing of tigers (gives a girl a big scare).*

The killing of tigers can be derived from two sources, e.g.:

(19) *The boy kills tigers.*

(20) *Tigers kill boys.*

It is quite reasonable to consider unambiguous constructions to be basic. The only question which remains is which is basic and whether *killing of tigers* is in fact really ambiguous. First, we must assume that whoever spoke (18)–(20) did not speak them without reason. Rules must reveal not only such reasons or causes, but also the order and stages of their taking place.

The following rules will serve the purpose of demonstrating how ambiguity is eliminated in terms of rules much earlier, before things evolve to the linear stage. These rules will also present our method of describing sentence formation. By applying certain conventions a formation takes place; one general convention, for example, is that rules apply progressively. Sometimes there may be conflicts which would yield non-grammatical constructions, but this is eliminated by establishing other conventions, to which the convention of progressive application must subordinate itself when there is conflict. All such conventions will be mentioned wherever necessary in the following rules.

13. Obt

13.1 Dit Aim

These two rules define object case. The item which functions as direct (Dit) aim (Aim) is called object (Obt). Case will be defined in a detailed grammar and object, locative, dative, subject, etc., will be given as cases. As we have stated before, case is the nominal item which directly participates in an activity (verb).

14. Subt

14.1 Actor

According to these two rules the actor (Actor) of an activity is called the subject (Subt) case.

Assume that there are two situations. In one the item 'boy' is felt as the actor, therefore as subject, and the item 'tigers' is seen as the direct aim, therefore the object of the activity item 'kill'. In the other situation the item 'tiger' is experienced as the actor, and therefore as the subject, while 'boy' is perceived as the direct aim, and hence the object of the activity 'kill'.

If the speaker has decided upon the functional relations (like object, subject, verb, etc.) for the given items, then this information is fed into the grammar which supplies from the lexicon the corresponding concepts like *tiger, boy,* and *kill.* We have used the term 'concept' here, rather than morpheme, to avoid entirely the notions of morphology. Sapir (1921) also used the term 'concept'. The lexicon will have lists of these concepts as shown below (only a partial list):

'Human, Male, Young, Boy, etc.' *boy*
'Animal, Male, Noun, Tiger, etc.' *tiger*
'Take life, Verb, Kill, etc.' *kill*
'Definite, Adje, Article, The, etc.' *the*

The semantic or meaning components are given first and the phonetic components, like *boy,* are given last. This convention implies that meaning must evolve before sounds. So long as this convention is understood it is possible, for convenience, to write the phonentic components first and the semantic description next, e.g.:

boy 'Human, Male, Young...'

Note that 'Boy' is one of the semantic components listed for *boy,* which implies that there may be many other meaning components composing the broad component 'Boy' of *boy.* While we may not be able to describe all those smaller components, nevertheless, evolutionarily we must assume their prior existence. The speaker is potentialy capable of being aware of all the necessary components of a concept.

The list of basic concepts increases as the individual or the linguistic community needs new concepts according to their situations. The speakers might invent new concepts for their new experience, or borrow from other languages, or from dialects of their own language. Grammar cannot, however, explain why one concept is borrowed, but not others. Similarly, grammar cannot explain why the item 'tiger' is represented by those sounds in that sequence, or why *tiger* cannot be made a verb whereas *man* can, as in *'They manned the ship...'*. Nonetheless there must be some principles of selection and linearity that determine the formation of a basic concept. Since we do not know how such principles operate, we simply assume all possible concepts listed with their semantic and phonetic components. But there is no doubt that every concept is the result of an experience and that the concept is reuseable whenever a similar experience takes place in the context of the items of a situation.

The items may be perceived with some modifications in their basic meaning. Since the items are now related to each by case rules, etc., the modificational concepts are clearly needed. Unlike basic concepts, modificational concepts are strictly limited and have to be associated with the basic ones by grammar rules. Thus it is unnecessary to list them in the manner of basic concepts. The following rules describe the modificational concepts and their grammar rules:

15. Sux   ——32

15.1 Devel, Eng...

These two rules mean that suffix (Sux) is a cover term for deverbal (Devel), ending (Eng), and a few other modificational concepts. The suffixes will be described through Rule 32. This is indicated by placing the number of the last rule in the rightmost corner. Thus 32 is placed at the right end of Rule 15. This convention means that the application domain of Rule 15 includes all of the rules from 15 to 32.

16. Stem——

A dash '——' after a symbol indicates the linear sequence of concepts. Here it means that the stem is followed by a suffix. The symbol Sux is taken as presumed after the dash:

      Stem——Sux

We have the general convention that the missing symbol on either side of any mathematical sign in use here is to be provided from the immediately preceding rule. By such ordered conventions we eliminate the repetition of the same symbols or rules. Similarly, we will have the convention that Rule 16 will apply only when a suffix has been selected. This is because, in an evolutionary sense, linear rules can apply only after elements have already been selected.

17. Devel   ——18

17.1 *ing...*

18. Stem = Vb

These three rules state that the term deverbal (Devel) covers suffixes like *ing*. The equal sign ' = ' is unidirectional and means 'is'. Rule 18 is within the domain of Rule 17; as a result the implication is that a Devel suffix's stem is a verb. But since the equal sign is unidirectional, it does *NOT* mean that a verb is a stem.

19. *ing* 'Progressive Act ÷ Stem'

This rule states that the suffix *ing* carries the sense of progressive act of its stem. Meaning or sense is enclosed in single quotes. The division sign ' ÷ ' means 'of'. There may be other kinds of sense in connection with the suffix *ing* and its stem, but we are concerned only with the present data of (18)–(20). Thus whenever the sense of progressive act of *kill* is needed, *kill* will be the verb stem for *ing*. Rule 16 applies to Rules 17–19 and places *ing* after its stem *kill,* yielding the sequence *killing.* As can be seen, we have a convention that linear rule can apply only *after* its corresponding selectional rule, no matter what the numeral order of these rules is. Accordingly, the convention that the higher number dominates the lower in a conflict is itself subordinate to the convention that a linear rule applies after its selectional rule. Thus, rules apply with conventions and conditions in an order and here such an order is called 'conditioned order'.

20.   ⊙ Noun

The unidirectional sign '⊙' means 'is like'. This rule states that the *ing* mentioned in Rule 19 is like a noun. The missing symbol on the left side of the ⊙ sign in this rule is *ing,* which appeared in the immediately preceding rule. This convention was discussed in the explanation given of rule 16. Once *killing* is considered as a noun it can be selected to correspond with a case item. This rule will not be needed if we imply that Act is always a noun.

21. *of* : Obt, Subt ÷ Devel Noun

This rule states that the preposition *of* occurs with the object and subject of the deverbal noun. Via Rule 20 the deverbal containing the form *killing* has become a noun and hence a deverbal noun; now the preposition *of* occurs with the subject or object of the deverbal noun *killing.* At this point it might be argued that Rule 21 makes *of* ambiguous, in the sense that it can occur with object as well as subject. How is this ambiguity eliminated in terms of rules? Actually, Rules 13–14.1 have already eliminated it. That is, according to 13–13.1, *of* occurs with the object of *killing,* which has been experienced as the direct aim (Dit Aim) of 'kill'. Similarly, *of* occurs with the subject of *killing,* which has been experienced as the actor of 'kill' by Rules 14–14.1.

The occurrence of the terms Obt and Subt in Rule 21 implies their definitions as were given in Rules 13–13.1 and 14–14.1 respectively. The definition rules are general and automatically apply to the defined term wherever it is employed.

It is clear from the rules that ambiguities like these are resolved much earlier and with fewer symbols than the TG rules which characterize them. The question, however, is not which approach resolves the problem earlier or later, or with more or fewer symbols. Our sole aim is to capture the essence or cause at the proper stage of evolution, no matter how many rules and symbols theoretically have to be exhausted. Practically, however, much fewer rules and symbols are required in our approach. We will now add the following rules to give a more complete picture of our method, so that we might go on to discuss some other very crucial questions of linguistic theory.

22. Eng

22.1 Inflen, Tee

The suffix called ending (Eng) covers two terms: inflection (Inflen) and tense (Tee).

23. Nol Bae : Inflen

A nominal (Nol) base (Bae) occurs with inflection suffix. The nominal base covers not only a noun base, but also a pronominal as well as an adjectival base. For example, *tiger* is a noun base and occurs with the plural (inflectional) suffix.

24. Vb 'Fine' : Tee

This rule states that a verb (Vb) occurs with a tense (Tee). An activity whenever experienced as complete or finite (Fine) will have its representative verb occuring with a tense suffix. The verb *kill* as seen in *kills,* for example, has the present tense suffix. For further clarification we wish to add the following sentences:

(21) *He kills those tigers.*
(22) *That boy kills them.*
(23) *They kill him.*
(24) *The boy eats sweet fruits.*

25. Inflen
25.1 prime, second...

The term inflection (Inflen) covers ending suffix classes like prime and second. Prime may also be called primary and second secondary. The word *tigers* in (20) has *s* as the representation of a prime inflection suffix, whereas the *s* of *tigers* in (19) is the representation of the second inflection suffix. These two occurences of prime and second become very clear when seen in the pronominal forms; thus *he* is with prime, while *him* is with second. Similarly, *they* is with *prime* and *them* is with second. However, it would be inconsistent to assume the differences in pronominal forms and not to assume them in other nominal forms, like nouns and adjectives. In later chapters we will find how consistency helps us to track down the diachronic route. Also, 'agreement' will be seen in the later rules of this chapter as the most important criterion for assuming the difference of prime, second, etc. It will also affect the word order.

Note that some symbols do not begin with a capital letter, e.g., the symbols prime and second in 25.1 begin with small p and s respectively. A symbol which does not begin with a capital letter is assumed to be directly represented by a phonetic shape (which may be zero). Rules 28 and 29 will directly replace these two symbols by phonetically overt and zero shapes.

26. Eng = second
27. If Bae ≠ Subt ÷ VB ÷ 'Fine'

These two rules state that the ending (Eng) is second class if the base (Bae) is not the subject of a finite verb. Note that Rule 27 is a conditional rule and applies to the immediately preceding rule. These rules imply that every base except the subject base occurs with a second ending inflection. Thus, the *tigers* of (20), *boy* of (19), *they,* and *he* have prime ending (inflection), since they are the subjects of the finite verb *kill.* But the word *killing* in (18) has the nominal base *killing* and takes the prime ending, because it is the subject of *gives.* The word *tigers* of (19) and (21), *girl* of (18), *boys* of (20), *him,* and *them* have second class inflections. These rules also imply that other nominal bases, such as the adjectives *big, the, a,* have either one or the other ending.

28. prime → *s* 'Pl' ÷ Noun Bae, ∅ Else

The prime inflection is replaced by *s* in the sense of plural (Pl) of a noun base (Noun Bae) and by zero (∅) elsewhere (Else).

This rule clearly implies that even the noun base in singular has a prime suffix, but it is replaced by zero. Zero implies here that the phonetic form of an entity has disappeared, but not the entity itself. Thus, *tigers* in (19) has the noun base *tiger* and *s* in the phonetic form of the prime suffix in the plural. The word *boy* in (19) has the noun base *boy* with a prime suffix with zero phonetic shape, since *boy* is not plural. Such pronoun bases as *he* and *they* also have zero phonetic forms of the prime class.

29. second →

This rule is restored as:

second → *s* 'Pl' ÷ Noun Bae, ∅ Else

That is, the missing symbols on the right side of the arrow are the same as those found on the right side of the arrow in the immediately preceding rule. This rule states that the second class ending suffix is replaced by *s* in the sense of plural of a noun base, but by zero elsewhere. The word *tigers* in (19) has the noun base *tiger,* with the *s* as representative of the second class inflection suffix. The words *him, them,* and *girl* of (18) have zero phonetic forms.

Zero phonetic shapes are well known in examples like *sheep* singular and *sheep* plural. We have consistently extended this same principle in our modified notion of endings. If we did not do so then it would be impossible to explain the agreement of verb and adjectives in sentences like *These big sheep are good,* as opposed to *This big sheep is good.* (See the rules of agreement below.) The point is that a suffix does not cease to exist simply because its phonetic form is absent in one context.

30. Tee

30.1 prt...

The symbol tense (Tee) is a cover term for symbols like prt tense. The term prt is not meant to be an abbreviation of 'present', but rather as a reminder that one of the meanings or functions of this symbol is 'present', which actually must be made explicit separately, as shown in the following rule:

31. prt 'Present'

One of the functions or meanings of the symbol prt is 'present'. Thus, prt is not present tense, but 'present' is rather one sense of it.

32. prt → s 'III Sir', ∅ Else

The prt tense suffix is replaced by s in the sense of third person singular (III Sir) and by zero elsewhere. The s in the word *kills* or *gives* is a phonetic representation of prt. The word *kill* in (20) has zero phonetic shape of prt since it is plural.

It should be noted that any suffix or phonetic shape which has been described so far is automatically placed after the corresponding stem by the application of Rule 16.

33. he → he (('Sir M' prime, *they* (('Pl' prime, *him* (('Sir M' second, *them* (('Pl' second

This rule lists the replacements of the third person pronoun base form with the various inflections. The duplicate parentheses sign '((' means 'with'. The form *he* is *he* with singular masculine (Sir M) prime inflection, *they* with plural (Pl) prime, *him* with singular masculine second, and *them* with plural second. Since pronouns, a subclass of nominals, display phonetic difference in four categories, e.g., *he, him, they, them,* then nouns and adjectives must also show this four-way grammatical difference. The substitution test offers one evidence that the speaker can distinguish nouns, for example, in these four categories. Otherwise it would be impossible for the speaker to know when to replace a noun by *he* or *him.* That is, *him* can substitute for a noun only when that noun can occur there with second class ending in the the sense of singular masculine. There would be more differences if the so-called genetive endings were also considered, but they have not been included in our data. Later it will be demonstrated how this principle leads us to the actual diachronic track through which these forms evolved.

34. *that* → *that* (('Sir' prime/second, *those* (('Pl' prime/second
The pronominal form *that* is replaced by *that* with singular inflections and by *those* with plural inflections. The slant bar between two symbols means 'or'. Since pronominal adjectives show difference overtly in singular and plural forms, we have to assume, for the reason of consistency, that all other adjectives, e.g., *big, a, the,* etc., are either singular or plural, with either prime or second endings.

35. Tee ÷ Vb :: prime ÷ Cae
The tense of a verb agrees with the prime ending of its case. The sign '::' means 'agrees with'. The agreement according to this rule implies concordance of person and number. Thus, *kills* is in agreement with *boy* in (19), because *boy* is a case having the prime ending. The words *they* and *kill* likewise agree, and so on.

36. Inflen ÷ Adje :: Inflen ÷ Sped
The inflection endings of an adjective agree with the inflection endings of the specified (Sped). Agreement in this rule refers to the concordance of the inflection classes. If the specified noun, for example, has the prime singular ending, then its adjective also has adjectival prime inflection in singular. This is true for second class inflections also. Thus, *those* is adjective for *tigers* and both have second class inflections in (21). In (22) *that* has prime inflection in singular, because its specified word *boy* has prime singular inflection. Similarly *a, the, sweet,* etc., agree with the nouns they specify as their heads.

From these two rules of agreement it is clear that agreement in English takes place in terms of endings. This fact is important for understanding the historical development of English.

37. s ÷ Eng → z) C_b, s)C_p
This rule changes the s of any ending suffix mentioned before to z after a voiced class of consonants, symbolized as C_b, and to s after a voiceless class of consonants, symbolized as C_p. Thus, the s of inflection is z in *boys* (after the voiced sound *y*). The same suffix is s after *t* (a voiceless sound of C_p group) in the word *fruits*. The tense suffix s is also replaced by z in *kills*, and so on.

After this there will be word order rules which apply only when all necessary words have been formed. Incidently, the definition of word will be given and discussed in the next chapter. The following rules describe the word order of the model sentences given in this chapter:

38. Word Order ——50

With this rule begins the series that describes word order. The domain of this rule is through Rule 50. It is implied here that the linear position described below is in terms of words, since Rule 38 has the symbol 'word' in it.

39. + Cae ((prime

The case (Cae) word containing a prime inflection ending occurs first; thus, *killing* in (18), *boys* in (19), etc., will be placed first, as they are the cases with prime inflections. Here ' + ' means 'Place now the following word'.

40. + Vb Main

The word that represents the main verb (Vb Main) is placed next. See *kills* in (19).

41. + Date

The dative (Date) case word is placed next as seen in (18), where *girl* is dative case. Dative *girl,* as in the *to a girl* type sentence, will be discussed in the next chapter.

42. + Obt

The object word is placed next. See *scare* in (18) or *tigers* in (19). Note that *tigers* of (19) has second class inflection, whereas *tigers* of (20) has prime class inflection, hence the difference in their position. Thus, it is clear that the endings do have a role in determining the position of a word in a sentence. This is another example of the evidence of smaller elements determining the behavior of larger elements. This fact is not revealed by the syntactic components of other approaches.

43. *of* Word Order ——46

The word order for the preposition *of* will be described below up to Rule 46. See Rule 21 which required the placement of this preposition.

44. + Promit

The word which is considered prominent (Promit) occurs first. In (18) the word *killing* is prominent, not *tigers,* therefore the first word to be placed is *killing.* This rule does not conflict with Rule 39, which has already placed *killing.*

45. + of

Then *of* is placed next, e.g., in *killing of.*

46. + Non-Promit

The non-prominent (Non-Promit) is placed next to *of,* e.g., in *killing of tigers,* where *tigers* is the non-prominent item. Note that the notion of prominence is also a matter of experience. It will be obligatory when we describe compounds in the following chapter.

47. Adje-Sped Word Order　　　　　——50

The order of the adjective (Adje) words and the words specified (Sped) by them is set by this rule and those which follow up to Rule 50.

48. + Arte, Pron Adje

Article (Arte) and pronominal (Pron) type adjectives are placed first. See the articles *the* and *a* and the Pron Adje *those* in the model sentences.

49. + Other Adje

Adjectives other than those mentioned in the preceding rule are placed next. See *big* or *sweet.*

50. + Sped

Then the specified (Sped) word is placed next. See *scare, fruits, killing,* etc.

In the TG approach a sentence such as (18), *the killing of tigers,* is considered an NP, which itself is a transformation of a base rule like $NP_1 + Vb + NP_2$, which characterizes the deep structure of (19) and (20). Thus, the TG method requires two stages of linear rules before *the killing of tigers* is understood—first, the base component rule stage and then the second or transformational component stage. In our approach Rules 13 and 14 decide the function or relation of the nouns which are reflected not only in (18), but also in (19) and (20). That is, our method implies that (18), (19), and (20) have *kill* and its cases derived commonly from one and the same source, which can be shown by the following figure:

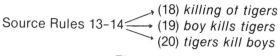

$$\text{Source Rules 13-14} \begin{cases} \text{(18) } \textit{killing of tigers} \\ \text{(19) } \textit{boy kills tigers} \\ \text{(20) } \textit{tigers kill boys} \end{cases}$$

Figure 2

In the TG analysis the (18) of Figure 2 is derived as:

Source Structure of (19)→(18)
Source Structure of (20)→(18)

Figure 3

In Figure 2 the cause of the three effects is one and the same, whereas in Figure 3 the effect is mistaken as the cause of another parallel effect. In simple words, the information of (18), (19), and (20) of Figure 2 originates not from one another, but rather from a common single source; because of this they look similar.

Now we might ask what are the advantages of our approach over that of TG? Our approach gives the information on subject-object and other case relationships much earlier and with fewer symbols, without resorting to any linear rules. Since linearity comes later in the evolution, we cannot establish an effective cause-and-effect relationship by maintaining that only a linear string can be transformed into another linear string. The fact is that a linear string is the result of many earlier non-linear decisions. For instance, Rules 13–14 are not linear, but because of them we observe relations like subject and object in the nominals. The linear arrangement of items and concepts takes place only when Rules like 13–14 have already been applied. Thus the TG formulation is overly simplistic; it not only fails to capture the cause, but even considers the effect as a cause. That is, TG misses the evolutionary direction and falsely assigns the origin of one sentence structure to another sentence structure. Notice that our word order rules are integrated in such a way as to obviate the use of two linear structures in order to prove that one is the base and the other is a transformation. This will be more apparent in the next chapter, when question and passive type sentences are included in the data. But we can see from Figure 3 that the symbols of linear structure in (19) are partially repeated in the linear structure of (18). This likewise happens when (20) is transformed into (18). That is, symbols on the right side of the arrow appear partly on the left side of the same arrow. On the other hand, in the integrated word order rules from 38 to 50 every symbol finds its linear place automatically, according to its status with reference to a given situation and selectional rules. In the integrated word order rules there is no need of pulling out a linear structure and repeating some of its symbols every time a T rule is applied to it. Moreover, it is highly questionable that the human brain would recognize the two interpretations of (18) by passing through the entire linear structure of (19) and (20), when it has the shorter route mapped by Rules 13–14, whose symbols are integrated with many others for linearity later in the word order rules.

We have observed here that the cause, when found at its main source, involves fewer symbols than when it is found at other sources, where many other elements begin to blur the causal relationship. It seems to be the nature of the human mind that it differentiates two elements at the point where minimum memory is involved. For example, consider the phonetic sequence [sʌn] which represents the concepts *son* 'the male child' and *sun* 'the star'. In the following sentence the listener may be confused:

(25) *That is our* [sʌn].

No one would, of course, seriously consider that (25) is derived from (26) or (27):

(26) *That is our* [sʌn] the star.

(27) *That is our* [sʌn] the male child.

The reason for not considering (26) and (27) as the sources of (25) is that *sun* and *son* are differentiated minimally at an earlier stage. That stage is the basic conceptual or lexical stage, where one meaning 'male child' and the other meaning 'star' are enough to distinguish one concept from the other in an evolutionary sense. The principle of minimal distinction at a non-linear stage is also the criterion for recognizing two sounds different from each other. Consider, for instance, the two sequences *bit* and *spit*. The root cause of recognizing *b* as different from *p* is that the former has 'voicing', while the latter does not. No linguist would ever use a linear criterion, i.e., would never consider that *b* was different from *p* because the latter could occur after *s,* while the former could not. It would be a double standard policy if we employed one principle in the case of two linguistic units, namely sound (or phoneme) and concept (or morpheme), but a different principle in the case of another linguistic unit, namely sentence. We need to consistently apply one and the same principle for distinguishing units of all kinds. This is the kind of consistency we use in locating the root causes of (18), not at the linear stage, but at the non-linear stage where the smallest distinction occurs. In other words, Rules 13–14 reveal the smallest distinction which would eventually affect the linearity of the corresponding concepts. It is clear then that two phonetically or linearly identical concepts, word or sentence formations are differentiated consistently at the non-linear stage.

This criterion of smaller and earlier distinction brings up another aspect of evolution—the evolution of a child's language. Does the child resolve ambiguities by means of linearization of various constituents? Or does he follow the order that is seen in the rules given in this chapter? We have indicated that situational relations are the most intrinsic and universal. For example, cases represent the same universal experience with regard to an activity irrespective of time and space in the synchronic or diachronic sense. Languages differ, however, in the expression of cases. It earlier was stated that even those humans who do not have the ability to use their vocal apparatus do have the ability to understand situational items associated with each other, in terms of basic functional relationships. We believe that a normal child is certainly endowed with the same ability. These functional relations are innate and need overt expression. Since humans employ sounds which can be produced only sequentially, the phase of linearity thus enters into the picture. So we first must describe those innate functions which relate the items of a given situation and associate those items with concepts that are gradually to be linearized. The child, because of this phonetic nature and its accompanying linearity, has to learn to express these functions or relations through linearization. It seems that the child picks up one or two items (a smaller number in the beginning) and attempts to indicate their functions without any linearity, because there is no linearity as such in the items of his situation. The functional relations, especially at the situation stage, are very few compared with the many linear positions for each function; the child takes time to master these positions.

Gradually more and more items and functions are expressed by the growing child, whose memory results in longer linear sequences. This simplicity in evolutionary growth is reflected in our rules. The more innate elements involving one function or relation at a time are taken up first, gradually heading towards linearity strictly in terms of ordered conventions. Had these innate functions or relations not existed in the thinking of the child, the question of linearity would not have arisen. In other words, linearity is the effect of non-linear aspects such as represented by Boxes A, B and C in Figure 1. It is, therefore, unnatural to resolve functional ambiguities on the basis of linear structures. We have stated before that it is basically the subject case function that places a noun before the verb in an English sentence like (18), (19), (20); it is not the placement that makes these nouns subject case.

If we accept this evolutionary reasoning, then the claim of the TG approach, that one base structure can be transformed into many others, is not correct. In several languages, the word order is so relatively rigid that it does mislead us into believing that, perhaps, one linear order of syntactic constituents is the base, with the others variations of it. English, for instance, has more rigid word order than many Indic languages. Reconsider sentence (6). This Sanskrit sentence can have any word occupying any position and yet their functional relationships do not change. Each word has inflectional suffixes indicating all necessary functional relations, like verb, cases, specifiers, agreement, etc. Because of inflections, however, this is often misunderstood to mean that languages like Sanskrit and Latin have free word order.

Staal (1967) has discused several generative aspects of Sanskrit sentences. It is sometimes argued that Sanskrit has no living native speakers and it is therefore difficult to ascertain intuitive matters in connection with word order. But consider Garhwali (one of my mother tongues) which, like other modern Indic languages, does not have as many overt phonetic inflections as Sanskrit. Yet the word order of Garhwali, while far more flexible than that of English, is not nearly as flexible as Sanskrit. Here is the Garhwali equivalent of the ambiguous part of that English sentence (18):

(28) *bāgū ku marnu....*

tigers of killing
'The killing of tigers...'

Following the TG method the deep structure of (28) would be found in a base structure like $NP_1 + NP_2 + Vb$, as exemplified by the following sentences:

> *naúnu bāg mard*
> boy tiger(s) kills
> 'The boy kills tigers'

and

> *bāg nauna mardan*
> tigers boys kill
> 'Tigers kill boys

Assuming that NP_1 is subject and NP_2 is object, we can represent the subject NP as N_s and the object NP as N_o. Then $NP_1 + NP_2 + Vb$ will be presented as $N_s + N_o + Vb$. The problem, however, is that a Garhwali speaker can present the same functional information, not only by the order of $N_s + N_o + Vb$, but also by $N_o + N_s + Vb$, and $N_s + Vb + N_o$, and $N_o + Vb + N_s$. That is, the linear positions may vary considerably. But then the analyst is forced to consider one order as the base. Such a consideration may not appear arbitrary on the surface, since the analyst might justify the $N_s + N_o + Vb$ order as being the most frequent and, therefore, the most basic. But statistical frequencies are not valid reasons for determining the base form. Unfortunately, the analyst, if he follows the TG notion, has no choice but to consider one order as the base, as I did in my earlier research (1966).

But a reader might reject this ad hoc or teleological justification on the grounds that the word order changes, but not the functional relations assigned to them. That is, whether it is $N_s + N_o + Vb$, $Vb + N_s + N_o$, or $Vb + N_o + N_s$, and so on, the elements subject and object (functional relations) still remain unchanged. Whatever was felt by the speaker as subject remains so, no matter what position the noun occupies in those changing orders. The same is true in the case of other nouns (object) and the verb (activity). Logically the constant factor is the functional relationship, not the word order. If the functional relations had changed with the change of word order, then there would be no possibility of communication, which after all is the sole purpose of language. So it follows that the element or factor which is constant is the base. We have shown by Rules 13–14 just such a constant factor. This logical validity is not found in TG analysis. And on top of that, where the word order is basically so free, the TG analyst is forced to resort to more and more arbitrariness.

Arbitrariness is further resorted to when we observe that, in TG base rules, first only one NP (the subject) appears (Rule 2) and then another NP (the object) appears (in Rule 3). In terms of linearity there is no evidence that one NP is more important than any other. Nor is it clear why NP_1 is not subsumed under VP, or why NP_2 has to be considered within VP. The fact is that if a situation needs an x number of cases for an activity, there is no way to tell which case emerged first, nor which case is part of the activity and which is not. When such evidence is not available, the only way left is to treat all the cases on a par. For those who rely on linearity, this means that they should present a verb and all its cases on the same line in one single linear rule, as is done in tagmemics at the clause level. For example, the tagmemic formula for an $N_s + N_o + Vb$ (Garhwali) sentence type would be:

$$tCl = S:N + O:N + P:tv$$

where tCl is the transitive clause, S is the subject, N is the noun, O is the object, P is the predicate, and tv is the transitive verb. Thus, the subject and object relations appear in one and the same formula.

It seems that the basic idea of constituent grouping is suggested by the old notion that a sentence consists of Subject and Predicate. Today's notion of rewriting a sentence in the TG approach as NP and VP is more or less patterned on that same old notion, with one difference. Terms like 'Subject' and 'Predicate' imply more intrinsic relationships than the linearized NP + VP type rules. Modern linguists often criticize the old grammarians for their notions based on Greek and Latin. One frequent accusation is that the old grammarians prescribed as universal that which they found, or thought they had found, in Latin or Greek models. Today, too, on the basis of the most frequent statement sentence types of modern English, the advocates of TG think that NP + VP is the basic rule for English and is universal for all languages. In reality such a view is prescriptive and is not needed for English, let alone for other languages.

There is no such thing as completely free word order, just as there is no such thing as completely fixed word order. Nevertheless, it is a fact that inflections do represent many functional relations in Sanskrit, Latin, etc. If so, then the order of descriptive rules require that we first state the functional relations, then inflections, then the word order. The reasoning is that functional relations are expressed through inflections and then inflections determine the nature of word order. The more phonetically overt one language's inflections are, the more flexible its word order and vice versa. In a language like English, where there are fewer inflections which have overt phonetic forms, the word order is relatively more rigid. Assuming that there is a language which has no inflections, it still has to have its concepts selected on the basis of functional relations. Only when all the necessary concepts have been selected and linearized can we proceed to word order rules.

However, the TG methodology has phrase order instead of word order. Even if we assumed that phrase is a unit of a sentence, no one can dispute that it is developed on the basis of linearity. One phrase may consist of other phrases. The problem is that in the base component there is no explanation available in terms of rules on how these phrases were suddenly linearized. Chomsky has shown that phrase structure (PS) rules cannot explain the linearity phenomena of many sentence types. He thought that a few PS rules which are linear could generate all the sentences of a language by means of T rules. But the question is what generates the PS rules? Whatever component generates PS rules probably is the same component responsible for generating the so-called transformed sentences. Semanticists tried to answer this question. They thought semantic rules were responsible for the base, with the base generating the transformed sentences, and so on. The semanticists, in their turn, began to ask about or deal with that issue which totally destroys the very purpose of language. The purpose of language is to express what a speaker experiences. Then the natural concern of a linguist or grammarian should be how best to describe those rules that enable the speaker to speak what he wants to. Instead the semanticists assumed the role of preachers. That is, they began to impose semantic choices on the speaker, which roughly means that you can choose only this semantic feature if you choose that one. They did not go beyond their semantics. They could have asked why, in the first place, the speaker cares to choose any semantic features? Did it not occur to them that there is something else before semantics begins? That something else is the creative aspect of language, not the semantic or syntactic component as falsely assumed by the followers of TG.

V

SYNCHRONIC METHOD

In this chapter a more detailed description of some model sentences will be given, in order to explain our method more fully. The model sentences were chosen in such a way that not only simple sentences or formations, but also some of the most complex ones, might be understood. The rules, when applied, assemble various elements and evolve them into more complex or next larger elements, leading ultimately to the formation of the model sentences. Every rule is provided with a subsequent explanation or cross-reference, unless it is self-explanatory. But sometimes a rule or symbol can be justified only after other rules have been given. The rules are ordered by means of certain conditions; there are some conventions which condition the order, therefore it is called 'conditioned order'. Some of these general conventions were mentioned earlier. They can also be regarded as rules which can be presented as shown below:

51. Progressive Application

This means that rules apply as they progress. There may, however, be conflict between two or more rules, in which case the following conventions are observed.

52. Dominant Rule ——53

The dominant rule order is given through Rule 53. Note that the domain of Rule 52 goes through Rule 53, as is indicated by the number 53 written to the right of this rule.

53. Latter Over Former; Internal Over External; Oby Over Opy; General Over Particular; Selection Over Linear

Rule 53 states that the latter or higher numbered rule dominates over the former or lower numbered one. Rule *b* is internal to Rule *a* if the former is within the domain of the latter. It is possible that *b* may be in conflict with *c*, which is outside of or external to the domain of *a*. In such a case, Rule *b* is still applicable within the domain of *a*. An obligatory (Oby) rule is dominant over a rule that applies optionally (Opy). In our description below, a rule is understood to be obligatory if the abbreviation Opy 'optionally' does not appear in its beginning. A general rule, such as a definition rule, dominates over a particular rule. A selection rule dominates a linear rule. Other conventions may be added whenever needed for particular languages. The conventions listed in that set order in Rule 53, however, are universal for the description of any language. These conventions allow rules to be presented sequentially. The application order of rules must reflect the direction suggested by Figure 1. Note that a semicolon indicates the progression order between the symbols on its two sides. Thus, theoretically the rule 'Internal Over External' will dominate the rule 'Latter Over Former', should there be a conflict between these two.

The following grammatical English sentences will be used as models in this chapter:

(29) *Those sweet fruits are given to her by that boy.*
(30) *She is given those sweet fruits by him.*
(31) *Every day they are given to her by the boy.*
(32) *That boy gives them to her and makes her happy.*
(33) *Every day he is giving those sweet fruits to a girl.*
(34) *That boy gives her them every day.*
(35) *Boys in Bengal kill tigers in those rough forests.*
(36) (i) *Is Ray a tiger killer?*
     (ii) *He could be (a tiger killer).*
     (iii)*He cannot be (a tiger killer).*
(37) *To kill tigers in the forests is not rough now.*
(38) *The girl is Miss Shiela Wilson.*
(39) *The boy is Wilbur and lives happy in Chicago.*
(40) *Now (you) send her the message by telecommunication*

   that Ray who kicked the bucket was an aggressor.
The sentences (36) (i)–(iii) are understood here as a single continuous discourse.

It is assumed here that the following rules in accordance with the aforementioned conventions are employed for the formation of these model sentences. At least one or two examples will be given to demonstrate the application of each rule.

54. Bac Conct

54.1 Nol Stem, Vel Stem, Adb Stem...

These two rules mean that the basic concept (Bac Conct) covers nominal (Nol), verbal (Vel), and adverb (Adb) stems. The dots '...' indicate that there may be more than these three types of stems.

The same numeral, when appearing in the following rule with a decimal point, indicates that the preceding is a cover term for the following. In this context the interpretation would be '54.1 is called 54'. The covered terms, e.g., Nol Stem, Vel Stem, and Adb Stem are within the domain of the cover term Bac Conct. Note that a covered term does not mean that it is an expansion of a higher or larger symbol. This kind of rule format has two purposes: one, to define a general term and two, to cross-refer or list several specific terms by a general name or cover term. Listing can be done by adding more decimal points, e.g., 54.2 for Vel Stem, and so on whenever necessary. Here we have used commas instead. Note that unlike a semicolon the comma does not indicate any order between the symbols on its two sides. Thus, Nol Stem could be presented after Vel Stem.

55. Nol Stem

55.1 Noun, Pron, Adje

The term Nol covers noun (Noun), pronoun (Pron) and adjective (Adje) stems. The noun stem in *fruits* is *fruit;* the Pron stem in *he* is *he;* the Adje stem in the word *sweet* is *sweet.*

A lexical entry of a basic stem, as shown in the earlier chapter (IV), includes in its semantic component terms like Noun, Pron, Adje, etc.

56. Vel Stem

56.1 Vb

A Vel stem is a verb (Vb). The Vb in *gives* is *give* and in *are* is *be.* One of the semantic components of the lexical entry of items like *give* or *be* would be Vb.

57. Vb

57.1 Acy Item

The term Vb is defined as an activity (Acy) item (Item). An 'item' is enclosed in single quotes in the examples below. In the situation of (29), etc., *give* is selected as Vb because it corresponds to an activity 'give'. Definitions like 57.1 imply the selection of concepts according to a given situation. That is, Vb, for example, refers to the item that is felt as 'activity' in a situation.

58. Adje

58.1 Noun Sper Item

An Adje is a noun specifier (Sper) item. The item 'sweet' is felt as a specifier of the item 'fruit' in the situation of (29).

59. Mol Conct

59.1 Sux...

The modificational (Mol) concept (Conct) includes the term suffix (Sux) and a few others, e.g., prefixes which do not occur in our model sentence. Every Mol Conct has to be described by grammatical rules, hence unlike a basic concept there is no need of listing it separately.

60. Nol Cae

60.1 Acy Partit Item

The term nominal case (Nol Cae) is defined as an item that is a participant (Partit) in the direct enactment of an activity (Acy). Case is a function by means of which an item is directly related to an activity.

61. Adb

61.1 Acy Sper Item

The item which is an activity specifier is called adverb. See the word *now* in (40) which has 'now' as a specifier of the activity 'send'.

62. Cae

62.1 Obt, Date, Loce, Inl, Subt...

The symbol case (cae) is defined as a cover term for these functions: object (Obt), dative (Date), locative (Loce), instrumental (Inl), subject (Subt), and others.

63. Obt

63.1 Dit Aim

The term object is defined as the direct (Dit) aim (Aim) of an activity. The word *fruits* represents the item 'fruit' felt as object in the model situations. Technically, it means that 'fruit' has the function of object.

64. Date

64.1 Ret

Date (Dative) is defined as the item considered to be the intended recipient (Ret) of an activity. See Rules 7–7.1 for further explanation. The item 'girl' in *girl* of (33) has the function of Date.

65. Loce

65.1 Time, Place

The locative (Loce) case covers the time and place items of an activity. The item 'day' in *day* is Time Loce, whereas 'forest' in *forests* has the function of Place Loce.

66. Inl

66.1 Means

Instrumental (Inl) case is that item which is experienced as the means of doing an activity. The item 'telecommunication' in *telecommunication* of (40) is Inl.

67. Subt

67.1 Actor

The term subject (Subt) refers to the item of the situation felt as actor (Actor) of the activity. The item 'boy' of *boys* in (35) is Subt case.

68. Sux

68.1 Devel, Eng...

These two rules state that suffix (Sux) is a cover term for deverbal (Devel), ending (Eng) and others.

The deverbals are those suffixes which occur with a verb, but not in the function of tense. Thus, *er* in *killer* is a Devel, whereas *s* in *kills* does not represent a Devel, since it expresses the function of tense. The words *kills* and *fruits* contain two types of endings, each represented by *s.*

69. Stem——

The symbol missing to the right of the dash '——' sign is brought from the immediately preceding rule, in order to restore the rule as:

Stem——Sux

This means that a suffix (Sux) is placed after a stem. See Rule 16 for full interpretation.

70. Bae

70.1 Come Stem

A base is a complete (Come) stem. It refers to an item minus the relations of word endings, e.g. *fruit,* not *fruits,* is the base. The adjective *sweet* completes the speaker's whole idea of the item 'sweet'; thus *sweet* is the base before the ending (phonetically zero). These two rules are the same as Rules 6–6.1, which explain the creative behavior of the person speaking, which is in turn responsible for the formation of even unprecedented stems. Base (Bae) also explains how speakers borrow from another language or dialect. That is, borrowed words actually first assume the form of base. There are other justifications, however, for the symbol 'base' which will become evident in later rules.

71.　　≠ Sux, Vb

The equal sign crossed by a slant bar '≠' means 'is not' (the opposite of equal sign ' = ') and is unidirectional. The term missing in the rule on the left of the unequal sign is the symbol Bae of the immediately preceding rule. Thus, this rule is to be read as:

　　　　Bae ≠ Sux, Vb
or　　　Come Stem ≠ Sux, Vb

This means that a Come stem is not a suffix or a verb. Thus, *fruit* in *fruits* is a base, because in this context nothing bigger than *fruit* can be a base stem. The verb *kill* in *kills* is not a base, nor are the suffixes represented by *s* in *kills* or *fruits* the base of this rule.

One should not get confused, however, if one were to hear a model sentence like *The s in the words fruits and kills is a suffix.* Note that the *s* (the first *s)* in the word *s* here is a base, but not the *s* in *fruits* or *kills*. The reason is clear. In this sentence the *s* of the word *s* is considered as a complete stem, hence a base, and it has zero phonetic representation in its singular. The sequence *mind you* has the base *mind you* in the following two sentences: *John often says 'mind you, mind you'. His 'mind yous' bother me a lot.* Neither the sequence *mind* as verb stem nor the suffix *s* of *yous* as pluralizer of the whole sentence *mind you* are bases.

72. Stem ((Devel = Bae

The stem with deverbal (Devel) is a base. Note that the equal sign ' = ' is unidirectional, which means that a stem with a Devel is a base, but not that a base is a stem with a Devel. The sign '((' means 'with' or 'containing'. The word *killer* has the base *killer;* neither the suffix *er* nor the verb *kill* is base. The stem is the verb *kill* with the Devel suffix *er.*

73. Devel
73.1 Parte, *er,* nfnt...
74.   : Vb

These three rules state that a Devel covers participle (Parte), *er,* infinitive (nfnt), and other suffixes; the Devel occurs with a verb (Vb) stem.

75. Parte
75.1 *ing, en*

The symbol Parte covers two suffixes: *ing* and *en.*

76. *ing* 'Progression'

The suffix *ing* has the sense of the progression of its stem, i.e., of a verb. This is observed in the word *giving* of (33). Rules like 19–20 will be added here if we have sentences like (18)–(20). Note that the modificational concepts are associated with a stem which requires change of the sense shown with the modificational concepts.

77. *en* 'Passivity' : Vb Tre

This rule states that *en* has the sense of the passivity of its stem and occurs with a transitive verb (Vb Tre). See the word *given* in (30), where *give* is the Vb Tre and *en* is the participle. In a more detailed grammar, *en* would occur in more than one sense, e.g., 'Perfect'. The better term for 'progression' is 'Imperfect', since that allows a parallel contrast with 'Perfect'. But this can be done only when we have included more detailed data. Note that the comma in a rule like 75.1 implies that only one symbol is to be selected at a time. Thus a verb, for example, can select either *ing* or *en* with a given concept at a time, but not both simultaneously.

78. *er* 'Subt' : Vb_{js}

The suffix *er* has the sense of subject (Subt) of its stem and occurs with a group of verb stems which we can list as Vb_{js}. The word *killer* has *kill* as the Vb Stem and *er* with it indicates subject. In this context *kill* is not a finite verb. The base *killer* gives the understanding 'the one who kills', by simply employing the symbol Subt; it also implies that it is a noun formation. It is clear here that the word or base formation is not based on some sort of syntactic structure. Thus the shorter evolutionary route for generating *killer* is to select *kill* by Rule 74 and *er* by 78. Then apply the linear rule 69 that places *er* after *kill.* The

structural explanation of *killer*, that as an embedded sentence
'X kills Y', is merely a kind of paraphrastic understanding of
Rules 74 and 78.

In a complete grammar there would be a list of stems called
Vb_{js} that could select the *er* suffix. The verb **aggress* would
appear in this list, where the asterisk indicates that such a verb
is inactive as a verb, but is activated when some modificational
concept like *or* is selected (where *or* and *er* represent only *er*).
The group listing can be presented separately from these rules
in the following manner:

G 1. Vb_{js}

G 1.1 *kill*, **aggress...*

79. *ion* 'Abstract Act' : Vb_{gs}

The suffix *ion* has the sense of abstract act of its stem and occurs with Vb_{gs} stems. The Vb_{gs} stems can be grouped in a like
manner to G 1 and G 1.1 above, where verbs like *communicate*
could be listed. This suffix is selected by *communicate* as
seen in *communication*. A verb may share more than one
group. For example, **aggress* would also appear in Vb_{gs} group
if we had *aggression* in our data.

80. nfnt 'Pure Act'

The infinitive (nfnt) suffix has the sense of purposive act (Pure
Act) for its stem. In the word *kill* of (37) there is nfnt suffix
which later will be replaced phonetically by zero. By employing
the symbol Act we imply that it is being changed to noun.

The nfnt suffix can occur with other functions, e.g., *be* in
(36ii), which has the nfnt suffix with the co-occurrent modal
verb *can* in the word *could*. This can be described as:

81. Vb Main : nfnt

82. If Cooct Vb = Modal

These two rules mean that the main verb occurs with nfnt, if
the co-occurrent verb is a modal. Note that a rule with 'if' in the
beginning always applies to the immediately preceding rule.
Thus 82 applies to 81. The modals too are selected according
to their sense corresponding to a situation. A classification of
verbs, therfore, is necessary and is shown below.

83. Vb

83.1 Vb Main, Vb Auxy

The symbol Vb covers two verbs: main verb (Vb Main) and auxiliary verb (Vb Auxy). The word *gives* has the main verb *give* and

the word *is* in (33) has *be* as Vb Auxy.

Note here that the term Vb has already been defined by Rules 57–57.1. Now Rules 83–83.1 use the term Vb again, in order to indicate that two types of terms, namely Vb Main and Vb Auxy, are referred to by the general term Vb. There is no conflict between 57–57.1 and 83–83.1. What it now means is that a Vb Main, for example, is a Vb and in turn refers to an Acy Item of 57.1. Thus, a term can be redefined or reclassified any number of times, so long as there is not conflict.

The term Auxy implies here that an auxiliary verb modifies the main verb, so as to indicate a certain modality or aspect of that main verbal activity. The following rule presents two such types of Auxy.

84. Vb Auxy

84.1 Modal, Aspe

The Auxiliary verb (Vb Auxy) covers verbs like modal (Modal) and aspective (Aspe). The word *could* has the modal verb *can*. The verb *be* in *is* of (33) is Aspe. Since modality and aspect refer to the main verb by means of auxiliary verbs, it is implied that the auxiliary verb is related to all other words in the same way as the main verb. For instance, the subject of the main verb *give* is *he* in (33) and, therefore, is also the subject of the auxiliary verb *be* in the same sentence.

The selection of an auxiliary verb, as has been said before, is motivated by the situation. For example, *can* is selected if the main activity is experienced with some abilitative mode (the sense of *can*).

85. Cooct = *be* Auxy

86. If Vb Main : Parte

The co-occurrent (Cooct) is the auxiliary verb *be* if the main verb occurs with a participle (Parte). In (31), *be* in the word *are* is Vb Auxy and occurs there because the main verb *give* occurs with the participle suffix *en*.

87. *be* Vb Main →∅

88. If Subt = Cooct ÷ Cooct Vb Main 'Fine'

The main verb *be* is replaced by zero if its subject is a co-occurrent of another co-occurrent main verb with the finite (Fine) sense.   ·

In (35) *Bengal* is not experienced as the locative case of the verb *kill*; rather its locative is *forests*. In a given situation a case can occur only when there is a verb. The verb for *Bengal* in (35) is *be*, which is deleted or replaced by zero because its subject is *boys*, which is also the subject case for the main finite verb *kill*.

89. Common Subt → Subt ÷ Vb 'Fine'

There may be situations where there is more than one activity, hence more than one verb. In such situations one verb may be finite and the other may be non-finite or deleted, but whose subject is common with that of the finite verb. Rule 89 replaces the common subject by the subject of the finite verb. The earlier evolutionary stage in (35) is:

boys be...boys kill

Rule 89 replaces the *boys* of *be* by the *boys* of *kill*. Note that *be* is deleted by Rules 87–88. Why *in Bengal* occurs after *be* will be explained later in the word order rules.

90. Compd   ——98

90.1 Bae_1 X Bae_2

The term compound (Compd) is defined as one base (Bae) felt to be in closest association with another base. The multiplication sign 'X' means 'in closest association with' or 'is compounded with'. It is impossible to know why some bases are felt to be compoundable while others are not. Certain general rules plus listing are necessary for taking care of the phenomenon of compounding. Rules 90–90.1 make a general statement that only bases (see Rules 70–72) can be compounded. The section for Compd goes through Rule 98. (See Appendix D also.)

91. Endoc   ——96

91.1 Compd Bae Refe ⟁ Member Bae Refe

The endocentric (Endoc) compound is defined as a compound in which the entire compound base reference (Refe) is equivalent to a member base reference (Member Bae Refe). In the compound word *tiger killer* the compound base is *tiger killer*, which is equivalent to a member base *killer*. The domination of Endoc goes through Rule 96. There are various other types of compound formations, e.g., exocentric compounds, not included in our data.

92. Obt X Stem ((Devel

This rule means that an object base is compounded with a base that has a stem with deverbal (see Rule 72). The base *tiger* is object of the verb *kill* in *killer*, which is a base composed of the stem *kill* plus the deverbal *er* (see Rule 63 for Obt). Because of this relationship between *tiger* and *killer*, the compound base *tiger killer* is formed.

This is another example of pinpointing the cause for the formation of a compound. We did not have to resort to superfluous paraphrastic structures like *NP kills tigers* → *tiger killer*; yet Rule 92 provides exactly the understanding which this T rule does.

93. Inl X ——94

This rule means that an instrumental (Inl) base is compounded with a Stem ((Devel type base. The missing symbol on the right side of the compound sign is provided by the immediately preceding rule, where Stem ((Devel is given on the same side of X. The compound *telecommunication* needs this rule plus the following one.

94. *tele* X *communication*

Rule 94 is within the domain of 93. This would imply that **tele* is felt as an instrument (see rule 66), like the base *radio* in *radiocommunication*, meaning 'communication by radio'. The difference is that **tele* appears basically as an inactive concept in the dictionary. This is indicated by the asterisk at the beginning of such a concept. Rule 94 activates **tele* when compounded with bases like *communication*. The base *communication* is also of the Stem ((Devel type. It is also possible to treat **tele* as a specifier (adjective) of *communication*, if it is not felt like *radio* in *radiocommunication*.

T rules can also be applied to compounds like *radiocommunication*. But this is done by resorting to strings like *NP communicates by radio*. They, however, fail to explain the **tele* because there is no possible string where *tele* could occur independently as *by tele*. In our method **tele* is compounded just like *radio* or any other equivalent base which is not basically inactive. Thus, consistency is here another advantage of our method. It may be argued by TG followers that the deep structures like *NP communicates by radio* provide the explanation. The fact is that such an explanation is provided by a shorter route as indicated by Rules 93–94. The aim, however, is not merely to find a shorter route. The shorter, or rather the shortest, route most probably starts where the real cause lies.

Rules like 93–94 resort to symbols which motivate not only the so-called deep structures as found in *NP communicates by radio*, but also the compound formations like *telecommunication*. Thus the evolutionary explanation, being more intrinsic, is also subtler. And the reason it is more intrinsic is because it reveals the cause at a much earlier stage than does a linear explanation.

In a detailed grammar there would be many other concepts like **tele* and *communicate* which would be grouped in the same manner as shown in the case of **agress* before. The rules then use group symbols on both sides of sign X.

95. 'Ancestor' X *son*   ——96
96. Compd = Proper/Family Name

These two rules state that a base in the sense of ancestor is compounded with *son* and such a compound is a proper or family name. In the compound word *Wilson* the base *Wil* has the sense of an ancestor (father, etc.) and is compounded with the base *son* in order to form a proper or family name.

The formation of compounded family names has recieved almost no attention in linguistic analysis. Yet no method can afford to neglect such important formations. There are many types of family names which must be described with evolutionary explanations. Rules 95–96 indicate that this can be done. Some names, however, cannot be explained in the manner of *Wilson*. For example, *Wilbur* may be a compound historically, but its historical bases, whatever they may have been, are beyond recognition at the descriptive stage. Such formations are simply listed as basic concepts. Thus, *Wilbur* appears as a basic lexical concept like Ray. This means that we cannot observe any sense in *Wil* and *bur* as being two separate concepts which are then associated in *Wilbur*. One might argue that the *Wil* of *Wilbur* is the same as in *Wilson*. This argument, however, is weakened by the failure to see any sense in *bur*. A basic concept consists always of a basic sense; the part *bur* must contain some sense in order to qualify as a concept or base. There must be some semantic history underlying *bur*. But historical semantic connections or conceptual derivations of which there is no synchronic awareness, are difficult to justify in a descriptive grammar. (For a different view see Lightner 1975.)

97. Bae$_2$ = Promit

In compounds the base (Bae$_2$) with which another base (Bae$_1$) is compounded is the prominent (Promit). Subscript numerals attached to the symbol Bae, Bae$_1$, and Bae$_2$ are meant to imply this relationship between the member bases of a compound. This means that Bae$_2$ in rule 90.1 is felt prominent.

98. Bae ——Promit

This rule places the prominent (Promit) base after another base which is not considered prominent. See Rules 44–46 also for further effects of this notion.

In compounds we have seen that it is not necessary for the two bases to preserve their basic meaning when they make a compound. For example, 'Mary' is a girl and is not a 'son' of 'Wil'. In order to resolve this problem, Rule 95 states that *Wilson* is a compound formed in the sense of 'family name'. This implies that a girl like 'Mary' can also belong to the family of 'Wilson'.

Idioms are the most interesting source for observing that words or concepts do not preserve their basic meaning when associated with other words or concepts. That is, they develop a secondary meaning. Such a development can be described in the grammar rules. The following rules make up the section on idioms where *kick the bucket* 'die' is described as an example of an idiom.

99. Vb = *kick*   ——102

100. Obt = *bucket*   ——101

101. Arte = *the*

102. 99–102 = 'Die'

These four rules state that the verb *kick* has the object *bucket*, which has the definite article (Arte) *the*. These three concepts are associated together in the sense 'die'. The lexicon already has the basic semantic and phonetic components of all the concepts of 99–101. The secondary development of these concepts in the form of an idiom is taken care of by 99–102. Later the word order rules will take care of the linearization of these concepts after they have been completed as words.

Note also that the secondary meaning of all the concepts from 99–101 is given in Rule 102 as 'die', which is an intransitive activity or verb. This means that it cannot occur with the sense of passive. Some verbs in English, however, may be basically transitive as well as intransitive, e.g., *run*. The verb *kick* is basically, i.e., lexically, transitive, but its secondary meaning in the idiomatic complex above does not remain transitive.

103. Word

103.1 Dee, Indee

These two rules define 'word', which is a cover term for the declinable (Dee) and the indeclinable (Indee).

104. Dee

104.1 Stem ((Multiple Eng

A declinable (Dee) is a cover term for a stem with multiple endings (Eng). The verb stem *kill* is seen with multiple endings, e.g., *kills* and *killed*, where *s* and *ed* represent the sense of tense ending suffixes. Both *kills* and *killed* are examples of declinable words. So are *boy* and *boys* in our model sentences. The bulk of English words are defined as words by these two rules.

105. Indee

105.1 Prepon, Conjun, Nege, Adb...

The indeclinable words are preposition (Prepon), conjunction (Conjun), negative (Nege), adverb (Adb), and others. There may be some words which have only one ending everywhere; such words can also be considered indeclinable. The prepositions like *to, by,* conjunctions like *and, that,* negatives like *not,* adverbs like *now* are all indeclinable words. So too it must be pointed out that what is indeclinable is highly relative. The concept *rough* as adjective in (35) is declinable, otherwise we cannot have sentences with *those rough forests* as opposed to *that rough forest,* where agreement takes place by means of number among the overt or covert endings. On the other hand, *rough* in *He plays rough* may be felt as an adverb and, therefore, cannot be differentiated by means of number, etc. It is thus indeclinable in this respect and may be considered to have one and only one ending (second ending according to Rules 111–112) throughout.

Some languages do not have a formal system of endings. In these, however, some sense would exist which completed the total relationship of a stem in a sentence. For example, a noun stem would be complete with its final relationship when its number, person, gender, or other relevant components corresponded to an item of the situation. This also applies to those languages where there are formal systems of endings. In English, for instance, *tigers* is with plural ending because there is the sense of plurality in the item 'tiger' in the particular situation. Grammar cannot account for the causes that determine why certain items are experienced with gender, number, person, etc. But grammar does account for the various kinds of endings which occur with the various stems. The maximum number of words can be defined as 'words' only via this sense of endings. The remaining number of words, like prepositions, is quite small and they are easily listed as words in a grammar of English.

The definition of the word is necessary for explaining the linguistic behavior of speakers. Every speaker is aware of the boundaries of the words he uses. He also knows the function underlying every word, otherwise he could not, for example, place them in order. Thus, the word order rules could not exist if 'word' was not defined prior to such rules. The following rules demonstrate how the majority of English words reach that stage of formation.

106. Eng

106.1 Inflen, Tee

See Rules 22-22.1 for the explanation.

107. Bae : Inflen ——108

A base (Bae) occurs with the inflection (Inflen) type ending. In (35), *tiger* is Bae and *s* is for Inflen.

108. Promit ÷ Compd = Bae

Rule 108 is within the domain of Rule 107. This means that the prominent (Promit) base of a compound (Compd) is the base that occurs with inflections. Rule 107 allows Inflen with any base. But 108 will allow Inflen with only the base of that compound which has been designated Promit in rules like 97-98. Thus, in a compound like *tiger killer* the Promit base is *killer* and, therefore, the Inflen will occur with it, not with *tiger.*

109. Vb 'Fine' ⫽ Devel : Tee

The finite verb without a deverbal suffix occurs with tense (Tee). The Sign '⫽' means 'without'. Because of new data this rule is a modified version of Rule 24. The tense will occur with any finite verb—main or auxiliarly—if it does not itself occur with Devel suffixes like participles, infinitive, etc. (See Rules 73, 81-82 and 85-86.) In (32) the main verbs *gives* and *makes* have tense suffixes. But in (33) the auxiliarly *be* expressed as *is* has the tense (see Rule 139), since the other finite verb *give*, which is main verb, also occurs with the participle (a deverbal) suffix *ing*. Similarly the tense is with *can*, not with *be*, in (36ii). That is, *could* is *can* with the *d* of pst tense and *be* is with the infinitive (nfnt) suffix, which is here phonetically zero.

110. Inflen

110.1 prime, second

See Rule 25 for explanation.

111. Eng = second

112. If Bae ≠ Subt ÷ Vb ÷ 'Fine'

These two rules are the same as 26-27.

113. Eng = prime   ——115

114. If Bae = Obt ÷ Vb ÷ 'Fine' (('Pase'

The ending is prime if the base is the object of a finite verb with the sense of passive (Pase). The domain of 113 includes 115.

The words *fruits* in (29) and *they* in (31) are objects, but they have the prime ending because the finite verb in these sentences occurs with the passive sense, represented by *given*. In *fruits* of (29) the prime class Inflen is represented by *s*.

115. Subt Bae : second

The subject base occurs with the second class of inflectional endings. Since Rule 115 is within the domain of Rule 113, the ending for the subject will be the second class ending whenever the object base occurs with the prime class ending. Thus, *boy* in (29) and *him* in (30) have endings from the second class, even though these two words have bases representing subjects (of the verb *give*).

116. Opy Eng = prime   ——118

117. If Bae = Date ÷ Vb ÷ 'Fine' (('Pase'

Optionally (Opy) the ending is prime if the base is dative case of a finite verb with passive sense. The word *she* in (30) is dative case, but it has the prime ending (represented by zero), because the finite verb has the passive sense (represented by *given*).

118. Bae ÷ Subt, Obt : second

The base of subject and object occurs with a second class ending. This rule applies only when Rule 116 operates. That is why Rule 118 is shown within the domain of Rule 116. Thus in (30) the object *fruits* and subject *him* have the second class inflections.

The term 'passive' does not seem to be satisfactory. The term 'active' should be interpreted as the experience in that situation where the actor is felt to be most important to the activity. 'Passive' should be replaced by the term 'objective', reffering to the situation in which the object is considered most important to the activity. In the context of English, the recipient (called dative) may also be felt to be most important to the activity and such a situation may be called 'receptive'. Thus Rules 116–117 could be revised as:

Eng = prime ——118

If Bae = Date ÷ Vb ÷ 'Fine' (('Rece'

which means the ending is prime if the base is dative of the finite verb, in the sense of receptive (Rece). Thus the term passive (Pase) in Rule 114 and elsewhere would be replaced by 'objective' abbreviated as Obje. The usage of Obje has the advantage of implying that *en* of 77, for example, would occur only when there is an object in the situation. Rule 77 can now be modified as:

en 'Objectivity' : Vb

119. prime → *s* 'Pl' ÷ Noun Bae, $\emptyset$ Else

120. second →

These two rules are the same as Rules 28 and 29.

The noun base *fruit* has the *s* of prime in (29), whereas the same base has *s* of second in (30) and (33). The pronouns here are considered with zero phonetic shape of prime and second, but *m*, for example, in *him* and *them* may be treated as equal to the *s* of the second. This is a matter for detailed description. There are many bases with the zero phonetic shape of prime or second ending in our model sentences. For instance, *given* is a stem with a deverbal, hence a base (see Rule 72). Thus *given* has a zero of prime class inflection in our examples. Similarly, *giving* is *give* with *ing* and zero prime inflection. All the adjectives, including articles, have either prime or second class inflections with zero phonetic shape. See Rules 149–150 for how the endings of deverbals and adjectives are determined by means of agreement. The word *kill* in (37) is the stem *kill* with infinitive (nfnt) suffix and zero prime inflection. The word *be* in (36ii) is also like *kill* in (37) as far as endings are concerned. Thus, except for indeclinables, all words of English, if they are called base, have inflectional endings. Even some indeclinables may be considered to have one and the same ending (which may be zero phonetically) in all contexts, e.g., *now*. But this is a matter for detailed description when more data has been given.

121. Tee

121.1 prt, pst, mprt

These two rules add two more tenses to Rules 30–30.1, namely pst and mprt beside prt. Just as prt is not employed to indicate only present sense, similarly pst is not only for past. The mprt tense is in the sense of 'imperative'. One tense may have more than one sense. Our data includes tenses with the sense indicated by the following rules.

122. prt 'Present'

This is Rule 31.

123. pst 'Past'

The suffix pst occurs with the sense of past. In (40) the word *kicked* has the pst suffix represented by *ed* and is in the past sense.

124. Opy pst 'Future'

125. If Stem = *can*

These two rules state that optionally (Opy) the pst suffix occurs in the sense of future, if the stem is the modal verb *can*. In (36ii) the word *could* has this verb with pst suffix represented by *d*. This means that *could* can occur not only to indicate 'past' by Rule 123, but also 'future' by Rules 124–125.

126. mprt 'Imperative'

The suffix symbolized as mprt occurs with the sense of imperative. In (40) the word *send* is a verb with this suffix whose phonetic components have been zeroed by Rule 130. In a detailed grammar there would be rules stating what auxiliary verbs could occur with mprt. For example, *will* in the sense of future of the co-occurrent main verb can occur with pst (as in *would*), or prt (as in *he will kill him*, where the prt with *will* is replaced by zero phonetic shape via the following rule). But modals like *will* and *can* do not occur with mprt suffix.

127. prt → *s* 'III Sir', ∅ Else

This is the same as Rule 32.

128. s ÷ prt → ∅ ((Modal

The s of the prt suffix is replaced by zero with a modal. There is zero with *can* in (36iii) in place of s for the sense of third person singular (III Sir).

129. pst → ∅ ((*be, ed* Else

The pst suffix is replaced by the phonetic shape zero with the verb *be* and by *ed* elsewhere. In *was* the verb is *be* with pst suffix represented by zero phonetic form. The word *kicked* of (40) has the verb *kick* with the pst suffix represented by *ed*.

130. cccc ÷ Sux Symbol → ∅

If the four lower case consonants (cccc) occur successively in a suffix symbol, then such a sequence is replaced by zero. There are two suffix symbols in our data which have been abbreviated with a sequence of four consonants, namely nfnt (for infinitive) and mprt (for imperative). This means that nfnt, as in *kill* of (37) or *be* of (36ii), is zero phonetically. Similarly, the word *send* of (40) has the verb *send* with mprt suffix symbol, which also has its phonetic components zeroed by this rule.

Note that the symbol Tee (for tense) covers three suffixes, namely prt, pst, and mprt. Since two members of Tee have partial phonetic representation as seen in Rules 127 and 129 it would be illogical not to assume a phonetic form for mprt as well, it being another member of the same suffix class (Tee). One member of a particular class can have zero phonetic shape, even if another member of the same class has an overt phonetic shape, i.e., is not zeroed phonetically. This logical consistency has been maintained throughout the description of inflectional endings (see Rules 119–120 and 28–29).

The same principle applies to the suffix nfnt for infinitive. This suffix is a member of the major class covered by the symbol Devel (see Rule 73). If some deverbal suffixes have overt phonetic shape, then we determine that the Devel suffix nfnt has a phonetic shape which is zeroed. In English we observe that whenever a verb is changed to a non-verb category there is some suffix associated with such a change. For example, the noun *killer* and deverbal *giving* are derived from the verbs *kill* and *give* by the association of the suffixes *er* and *ing* respectively. This means that the infinitive *kill* in (37) must also be considered as derived from the verb *kill* with the association of a suffix; that suffix is nfnt. If we do not accept this description then we are not consistent in logical terms. In the following chapter we will find how necessary this logical consistency is as a tool for seeing the diachronic reality.

This logical principle, however, does not apply to a formation which has two or more basic functions in its lexical description. For example, the concept *rough* has two basic functions, as either adjective, e.g., in (35), or as adverb in a sentence like *He plays rough.* One basic function cannot be a derivative of another basic function. A lexical entry lists only those meanings or functions which are considered basic.

131. $s \div$ Eng $\rightarrow s$) C_p, z Else
This rule was explained before as Rule 37. Note that this rule does not imply that the *s* of *gives* and the *s* of *boys* are one and the same suffix. It simply states that the ending suffixes represented by *s* undergo the change given in 131.

132. $t \rightarrow š$ ($i \div ion$ ——133
The *t* is replaced by *š* before the *i* of *ion*. The suffix *ion* of 79 has the palatal vowel *i* which is a factor in replacing the *t* with *š*. Thus *communicate* ends in *t* which is replaced by *š* according to this rule

133. $i \div ion \rightarrow \emptyset$
Since Rule 133 is within the domain of 132, the replacement of the *i* of *ion* by zero takes place after 132 has been applied. Thus, the *i* is zeroed after *t* of *communicate* has been replaced by *š*. Thus, *ion* implied as *iən* remains *ən* by this rule. Actually more data will modify these rules.

134. Sente

134.1 Set ((Tee
These two rules define sentence (Sente) as a set (Set) with a tense (Tee). All of our model sentences fall in this type of definition. No sentence is complete without a tense. Tense occurs only with a finite verb which may be a main or auxiliary verb. A verb implies its cases, adverbs, etc. The cases, in turn, imply other possible adjectives as required by a given situation. Thus these two rules imply the entire build-up. For example, *gives, is, makes,* etc., occur with a tense, without which the sentences could not be considered complete; these verbs refer to a situation where there are case items and specifiers (adverbs, adjectives, etc.) which are directly or indirectly

related to these verbs.

There may be sentences which represent a complex situation, i.e., a situation having more than one activity or verb. For example, (37) or (40) represent complex situations. In (37) we see two activities reflected by the verb stems *kill* and *be* (of *is*). In (40) *send, communicate, kick,* and *be* (of *was*) represent an even more complex situation. Sentence (35) is also complex even though the verb *be,* of which *Bengal* is the locative case, has been deleted. There may be other types of sentences in a language; they can be defined likewise or with other suitable definitions.

135. *he* → *he* (('Sir M' prime, *they* (('Pl' prime,
        him (('Sir M' second, *them* (('Pl' second,
        she (('Sir F' prime, *her* (('Sir F' second

This rule indicates changes in the stem of *he,* which would be listed in the lexicon as a concept meaning 'third person pronoun'. See Rule 33 for its further explanation. The changes are due to the differences of number, gender, and inflectional endings. For example, *he* is *he* with singular masculine prime inflection, but is *she* with singular feminine (F) prime inflection. We assume here that a pronoun is understood to refer to a noun in those respective categories (e.g., singular, masculine, prime, etc.).

136. *that* 'Adje' → *that* (('Sir' prime/second, *those* (('Pl' prime/second

This is the same as Rule 34.

Thus *that* is listed in the lexicon as a pronominal adjective as well as a conjunction. The *that* of this rule occurs in the sense of adjective, since the symbol Adje appears above after *that.* It is also possible to consider the adjective meaning or function of *that* as basic and the conjunction meaning secondary. If so, then a rule would be required in the grammar to indicate that *that* also functions as a conjunction. Note, too, that in English conjunctions are indeclinables, while adjectives are declinables.

137. *who* → *who* ((prime

The third person relative pronoun *who* is replaced by *who* with prime inflection. With additional data there would be more stem changes as we added categories like neuter to those of masculine and feminine. Pronouns which do not change stems for these categories do not need rules such as 135, 136 and 137. Their basic description is available from their lexical entries.

138. *an* 'Arte' → *a*) C

The article (Arte) *an* is replaced by *a* before consonants *(C).* For example, *an aggressor,* but *a* before *tiger.*

139. *be*→ *i* ((ʻIII Sirʼ prt, *was* ((ʻIII Sirʼ pst, *are* ((ʻPlʼ prt, *be* ((nfnt

The verb stem *be* is replaced by *i* with third person singular prt tense as in *is,* by *was* with third singular pst tense, by *are* with plural prt tense, and by *be* with nfnt (infinitive) suffix as in (36ii). Note that the stem in *is* is *i* with the *s* of the prt tense suffix (see Rule 127). The stems *are, was,* and *be* occur with other respective suffixes whose phonetic forms are replaced by zero. Thus see Rules 127, 129–130.

There are other suffixes and basic concepts which might require some overt phonetic changes if more data were added, e.g., the participle *en* (see 77) is replaced by *ed* with other types of verbs, as in *are killed.* Otherwise, given our data it is implied that *en* remains *en* if no change rules like 131 are added. We will assume that here all such changes are taken care of in the manner of the rules given above. All other basic information (semantic and phonetic) is presumed in the lexical entries of a basic concept.

140. Prepon

140.1 *to, by, in*...

A preposition (Prepon) is a cover term for *to, by, in,* and others. It is possible to not give this rule in the grammar if preposition is considered a basic function of concepts like *to, by,* etc. The reason for such a decision might be the fact that these concepts could occur as basic concepts, e.g. *in* in the sentence *Come in!* If *in* was basic then we would have to assume that *in* was a base occuring with an inflection ending. But instead these concepts occur as prepositions in our data. And they must be considered words, whether by assuming they have an ending or by listing them as words. (See Rules 105 and 107.)

141.   : Word ——145

This rule states prepositions occur with a word. This rule dominates through 145.

142. *to* : Date ((second, Stem ((nfnt 'Pure Act'

Because of additional data this rule is a modification of Rules

7–8. The preposition *to* occurs with a dative case word contain- ing a second class inflection ending. See *to* with *girl.* The word *her* in (31) is dative with second class inflection and, therefore, *to* occurs with it. However, *she* in (30) is also a dative word, but is with the prime inflection ending; thus *to* cannot occur with it. See also Rules 116–117. In (37) *to* occurs with the word *kill,* which has the stem *kill* with the infinitive suffix (nfnt), in the sense of purpose (Pure) act of its stem (Rule 80).

Note that *girl,* for example, must be a word functioning as dative case before *to* is selected. Since a preposition is a word according to Rule 105, it will not be placed with *girl* like an af- fix. The assignment of the status of word to a preposition and its co-occurrent makes a difference in the word order rules to be given later. For example, later *to* will be placed before *a* as in *to a girl,* which is possible due to the fact that all three, namely *to, a,* and *girl* have been declared words by previous rules. Moreover, since Rule 142 is within the domain of 141, the Date is implied to have the status of word.

143. *by* : Subt ((second

The preposition *by* occurs with the subject case word that is with a second class inflection ending. See *by* with *boy* in (29). That is, *boy* is the subject, but is with second class inflection like *him* in (30). Rule 143 selects *by* for *boy* in (29) and for *him* in (30). The word *boy* in (32) or *he* in (36) are also subject case words, but *by* cannot occur with them since they are not with a second class ending. See Rule 115 for the cause of second class ending with *boy* of (29) or *him* of (30).

144.   : Inl

The preposition *by* occurs with an instrumental (Inl) case word. See *by* with *telecommunication* (the instrumental case word for the verb *send)* in (40). Note here that *by* does not occur with the base *tele,* the base *communication,* nor with the base *telecommunication,* but only with the whole word *telecom- munication.* See Rule 66 for Inl.

Incidently, Rule 144 is not needed if 143 is presented in the manner of 142, e.g.: *by* : Subt ((second, Inl

But we do not save any symbols this way. On the other hand, because of more data we may eventually need the separate reference or operation of *by* with subject or of *by* with in- strumental. Then two different numbers like 143 and 144 will be helpful. We have already indicated before that rule numbers do not count as symbols. The numbers are needed only for reference so that the operation of the rules can be understood conveniently.

145. *in* : Loce ⫫ *every* 'Adje' ÷ *day*

The preposition *in* occurs with a locative case word. See *Bengal* or *Chicago* where *in* occurs with these locative case words. Refer to Rule 65 for Loce. This rule states that such a locative word should not be *day* with *every* as its adjective. Thus, *day* in (31) is a locative word whose adjective is *every* and this prevents the preposition *in* from occurring with *day*.

146. Sente 'Content' : *that* 'Conjun'

147. If Cooct Sente : Word 'Contentive'

The sentence (Sente) as content occurs with the *that* conjunction (Conjun) if the co-occurrent sentence occurs with a word in the sense of contentive. The understanding here is that there is a situation in which one sentence is experienced as the content of a sentence that contains a contentive word. Such concepts as *message, fact, idea, claim,* etc., have basically a contentive meaning. Also, some verbs have this basic sense, e.g., *say, call, consider, decide,* etc. The semantic complex of such concepts lists 'contentive' as one of the components in the respective lexical entries.

In (40) the sentence *that Ray was an aggressor* is experienced in the sense of content for the sentence *Now (you) send her the message by telecommunication,* which contains the word *message.*

148. Coord Sente : *and*

A coordinated (Coord) sentence occurs with the conjunction *and,* where there is a situation which is experienced as coordinated with a prior situation. Two or more such situations are represented by this rule. The sentence that represents a coordinated situation is a coordinated sentence. In (32) we have to assume that the coordinated sentence is *that boy makes her happy.* Later Rules 151–152 will delete the first two words of this sentence.

149. Eng ÷ Vb 'Fine' :: prime ÷ Cae

This rule states that the ending of a verb having the sense of finite agrees with the prime ending of a case; it is a slight modification of Rule 35 because of the additional data. Thus the tense ending of *gives* is in agreement with *boy* in (32), because *boy* is a case having the prime ending. In (29) and (31) the tense in *are* agrees with *fruits* and *they,* which are the object cases with prime ending, whereas in (30) the tense in *is* agrees with *she,* which is the dative case with prime ending. Rules 111–118 explain the reasons for the occurrence of prime with various cases. The endings of *given* and *giving* are prime (with zero phonetic shape by 119), because they agree with the case words which have prime ending. The deverbal *be* with nfnt has prime ending in (36ii), because *he* has the prime ending, whereas *could* in the same sentence has *d* representing third person singular pst tense. That is, agreement in English implies concordance of person and number.

150. Inflen ÷ Adje, Prede Nol :: Inflen ÷ Sped

This is the same rule as 36 with two additional symbols, namely predicate (Prede) nominal (Nol). The example of Prede Nol is *happy.* In (32), *happy* agrees with *her* in ending, because the former is the predicate for the latter. In (39) *happy* is predicate for *boy* and, therefore, the former has the prime inflection agreeing with that of the latter. The word *rough* in (35) is an adjective whose specified (Sped) word is *forests.* Since *forests* has the second class ending it is, therefore, assumed now that *rough* also has the second class ending (phonetically zero by Rule 119). On the other hand, since *kill* of (37) has prime, its predicate adjective *rough* too has to have its own prime ending. But *rough* as an adverb, e.g., in *He plays rough,* is considered to have one and only one ending, which by Rules 111–112 is a second class ending.

It is now clear that agreement in English takes place in terms of endings. In the evolutionary order the agreement can happen only after the functions of the base are known. This is why Rules like 111–118 must apply before 150. In the next chapter it will become explicit just how important this fact is to the understanding of the historical development of English.

151. Opy Same Word // In Equip // ÷ Sente$_f$ → $\emptyset$

152. If Sente$_f$ = Coord, Answer... ——153

These two rules state that optionally (Opy) the same word of a following sentence (Sente$_f$) which is in equi-membership (Equip) is replaced by zero, if the following sentence is coordinated (Coord) or is an answer (Answer) of a prior sentence.

The prose explanation in a rule is enclosed in double slant bars '*//*'. In (32) we have to assume that there was an earlier stage at which we had two sentences:

(a) *That boy gives them to her.*

(b) *That boy makes her happy.*

Here (b) represents the situation that was experienced as an addition to (a) and, therefore, the sentence representing the situation underlying (b) is called the following sentence (Sente_f). The speaker might experience the situation of (b) as coordinated or linked with that of (a). The words *that boy* of (b) are the same as the words *that boy* of (a) in every aspect. That is, *that boy* of (a) and *that boy* of (b) are in equal membership (equi-membership). More explicitly, *that boy* is related to *makes* of (b) in the same way as it is related to *gives* of (a) in (32). By these two rules, therefore, the *that boy* of (b) is deleted. The result is:

(a) *That boy gives them to her.*

(b) $\emptyset$ $\emptyset$ makes her happy.

The answer type situation is discussed with the following rule.

153. Opy Pron Subt, Vb Main $\not\rightarrow$ $\emptyset$

By this rule the pronoun subject (Pron Subt) and the main verb are not deleted. The arrow crossed with a slant bar means 'is not replaced by'. Rule 153 is within the domain of 152. We have assumed here that (36i–iii) is a continuous discourse. These three sentences have common words with the identical relations or functions, that is, with equi-membership. Rules 151–152 delete all such common words of (36ii) and (36iii), as they are answers to (36i). Rule 153, however, keeps optionally the pronoun subject *he* and the main verb *be* in (36ii–36iii). The auxiliary verb *can* and negative *not* are not in (36i) and, therefore, they are in (36ii) and (36iii).

154. Opy Pron Subt $\div$ Vb ((mprt $\rightarrow$

This rule means that optionally the pronoun subject of a verb with imperative suffix is replaced by zero. The symbol '$\emptyset$' is supplied from the preceding rule, where '$\emptyset$' appears on the right side of the arrow. In (40) the pronoun subject is *you,* which may be deleted because the verb *send* is with the mprt suffix in the sense of imperative (see Rule 126). Note that the agreement rule (149) occurs before this rule, which means the ending of the verb *send* of (40) has already been selected on the basis of the ending of *you*. Thus, it is very clear here that there is an evolutionary order in which events take place.

155. Word Order ÷ Sente ——171

The word order rules begin here and go through Rule 171. See also Rule 38 for more explanation. This word order takes place within the limits of a sentence, as indicated by Sente in the rule. The sign ' + ' places a word.

156. + Conjun

This rule positions a conjunction (Conjun) word. The word *that* belongs to the sentence *Ray was an aggressor* by Rules 146–147 and Rule 156 places *that* in the beginning. See also *and,* which is placed first in the sentence *makes her happy* of (32) or *lives happy in Chicago* of (39). The deletion of other words in these sentences is described in Rules 151–152.

157. + Adb 'Time'

The adverb word in the sense of time is placed next. In (40) *now* is the example. It is possible to consider this rule optional, like the following one.

158. Opy + Loce

Optionally the locative (Loce) case word is placed next. The word *day* (31) or (33) is an example. The adjective *every* will be placed before *day* by later rules.

159. + Vb *be* ÷ Sente 'Confe Q'

The word containing the verb *be* of a sentence, in the sense of confirmative (Confe) question (Q), is placed next. Confe Q implies a 'yes or no' type question. The *be* of *is* in (36i) is an example.

160. + Cae ((prime

This rule is the same as Rule 39. Notice that *kill* in (37) is the subject case with prime ending (*to* will be placed by a later rule). The word *she* is dative case, but with prime ending according to Rules 116–117. So *she* is placed there instead of the subject *him,* etc., in (30). Similarly, *fruits* in (29) is the object case word with prime ending by Rules 113–114. So *fruits* of (29) or *they* of (31) are placed first, not their subject word *boy.* Adjectives will be placed before a case word by later rules.

Thus it is evident that the English word order works not only in terms of cases, but aso in terms of what kind of ending a case has. In the next chapter this point will be emphasized more. But it must be noted here that the descriptions of

English syntax modeled after some current approaches have missed the real causes or motivations of word order changes as shown in this rule.

161. + Vb Auxy, *be* 'Vb Main'

The auxiliary verb is placed next, e.g., *is* in (30). The *be* of *is* in (37) is the main verb.

162. + Nege

A negative is placed next, e.g., *not* after *can* in (36iii) or after *is* in (37).

163. + Vb Main

Main verb examples are *given* in (29), etc., *be* in (36ii), (38), etc., and *send, kicked,* and *was* in (40). Note that *be* as main verb already has been placed in (37) and (40) by Rule 161. Now Rule 163 places other main verbs. Since *kill* in (37) is a main verb, for its case words also, like *tigers,* we must assume that 163 has to apply. Rule 160 too applies to *kill* of (37), since it functions as a case with prime ending. Thus two rules can apply to one and the same word, because such a word has two functions, one as an activity and the other as a case for another activity, which is the verb *be* of *is* in (37). In (35) the deleted main verb is also *be,* the locative case of which is *Bengal* (see Rules 87–88). We have to assume that *be* is placed there as zero after *boys* and before *in Bengal.* The point is that case words, etc., are placed with reference to their respective verbs.

164. + Prede Nol ÷ Subt ((prime

The predicate nominal (Prede Nol) is placed next. See *rough* in (37) and *happy* in (39). The *happy* of (32) will be taken care of by Rule 167 since it is the predicate nominal for *her* which contains a second class ending. That is, in (39) *happy* is the predicate of *boy* which has prime ending. Rule 164 still applies if *happy* is felt as an adverb (the specifier of a main verb by Rules 61–61.1) for *lives* of (39). Note that adverbs like *roughly* or *happily* are derived from their adjective base, not from the adverb base, which is also listed as a basic semantic component of the adjectival concepts.

As a side note, it is an interesting point that Rule 164 will also take care of the predicate *happy* in a sentence like *She was made happy,* by writing Obt after Subt in this rule (because *she* has the prime ending).

Since the placement of *happy* partly varies from the derived adverb *happily,* it is necessary to make a difference between a predicate nominal and an adverb. The concepts like *happy* or *rough* would, therefore, be considered here nominal with an optional function of adverb. This can be indicated in their lexical entry by writing 'Opy Adb' (optionally adverb). The rule for *happily* type adverbs will be different from 164.

165. + Date ((second

The word representing the dative (Date) case with the second class ending is placed next. In (34) or (40) *her* is a dative word with the second class ending (see 120 and 135). Rule 165, therefore, places it after the main verbs it refers to as its activity. It is possible to make this rule optional; note that *she* in (30) is dative with prime ending, hence this rule does not apply there.

166. + Obt ((second —167

The object case word containing a second class inflection is placed next. In (32) or (34), *them* is the object case which is placed there by this rule. See also *message* in (40) for another example. Rule 167 is under 166.

167. + Prede Nol ÷ Obt ÷ Vb 'Fine'

The predicate nominal of the object case (of 166) of the finite verb is placed next. In (32) *happy* is a predicate nominal (adjective) that is a specifier of *her,* which is the object case (of *makes)* with the second class ending. A sentence like *Ray the tiger killer was an aggressor* (not in our data) has a sequence *the tiger killer,* functioning as a predicate which is derived from *Ray is the tiger killer,* where via Rule 87 the *be* of *is* is deleted or replaced by zero.

Rules like 164 and 167 imply that Prede Nol are possible only for the subject or object in the circumstances stated in such rules. It does not mean, however, that Prede Nol will be placed after an object case word which is preceded by a dative case word. This is because we do not have a situation where a Prede Nol is experienced for an object that occurs with a dative. This principle of situation applies to all the placements or linearizations of words. The word order rules aim at integrating all such placements with optimum generalizations. Such generalizations automatically eliminate the need of many separate rules which involve repetition of the same symbols again and again.

168. Opy + Date ((second

This rule is the optional (Opy) placement of the dative case word containing a second class ending next. See *her* in (32) or *girl* in (33).

In our situation there is only one dative case item, namely 'girl', which is represented by *girl,* as in (33) or *her,* as in (29) or (40). Hence this dative word can be selected only once and, therefore, can be placed only once in the sentence, either before the object word by Rule 165 or after it by Rule 168. A speaker may place any word more than once due to some memory loss or other psycho-physiological problem, but this does not mean that there are really that many corresponding items in the situation, unless one and the same item can be experienced in more than one relation or function. The grammar rules would account for such an experience anyway, if it were to happen in actual situations.

169. + Subt ((second

The subject case word containing a second class ending occurs next. See *him* in (30) or *boy* in (29) or (31).

Here we observe clearly the advantages of integrated word order rules. For example, Rule 169 simply places the so-called passive subject after the verb, without involving the repetition of the same symbols several times over. Suppose we follow the old TG belief that the passive is a transform of active; then we first present the structural rule of active, like (c) NP_1-Aux-V-NP_2, and then apply the T rule in order to generate (d) NP_2-Aux + be + en-V-by + NP_1. What happens here is that all the symbols of (c) are repeated in (d). That is, the symbols NP_1, Aux, V, NP_2 occur in the active and are repeated in the passive. Our rules are ordered, integrated; therefore, such repetition is not possible. Most importantly there is evidence that every passive does not have an active counterpart and vice versa in many languages. In the TG approach it is implied that if the active sentence is a possibility, then the passive is also a possibility. The serious question is whether this means that the human mind or brain operates on passive only after recognizing its active counterpart. A common sense argument would be that the operation would rather take place via the shorter route. That is, the speaker can decide right in the beginning whether a situation is with active or passive sense. If it is with active sense it would operate directly on the active; if it is with the sense of passive, then it directly would operate on the passive. It is in the interest of evolutionary economy that the mental process would not go to passive via the route of active. Our rules suggest just such an efficiency of mental operation.

TG rules like (c) and (d) imply that passivization takes place linearly from its active base. This is another serious question of whether the generative process really begins with linearization. The hearer does receive information linearly. But we are talking about the generative process where the speaker is involved. Our view is clear; linearity comes much later, after such decisions have been made as to what functions and relations the situational items have and these decisions have been assigned by the speaker. Even if the speaker does not linearize and, therefore, does not speak a single word, the situation as viewed by the speaker still exists. Thus, this inner composition of a situation, and ultimately of a sentence, is far more important than mere linear identification of the constituents of sentences.

The other drawback of (c) above is that it does not reveal the essential cause that selected NP_1 and placed it there in the first place. In our approach one can go back and find out why the subject case needs a second class ending (Rule 115). Rule 169 implies that because of the second class ending this subject cannot be placed like the subject with prime ending. These changes did not come to modern English arbitrarily. The role of endings in influencing the so-called syntactic changes is not revealed by TG rules. That is, the TG approach is not powerful enough to give us insight into the evolutionary reasons for the difference in the placement of one and the same noun. Thus, the TG rules may have the advantage of quick readability, but we gain no evolutionary insights synchronically or diachronically.

From this discussion it is clear that the rule format of TG is not adequate to continue the so-called base structures and their transformation in one and the same order as far as possible. For example, consider the question sentence (36), the conjunction sentence (40), the predicative sentence (32), the passive sentence (29), the dative passive sentence (30) etc. Each of these sentences would be described with a base structure and then a transformed (surface) structure. This involves a tremendous waste. On the other hand, our rules integrate as many sentential symbols in a continuous order as possible. The speaker, then, is expected to linearize the corresponding words in that order. Note very clearly that in our theory concepts are selected not because there are concepts, but because there are certain items in a situation which have certain relationships. Thus, the situation controls the words of the sentence by referring to those items. Otherwise one might reach a wrong conclusion that our integrated word order rules produce odd sequences, as in sentences like: *That now every day is not John made happy;* or, *But now every day the boy gives her fruits to her.* We require as essential the condition that a speaker is conveying a situational view. If that view is not represented by the produced sentence, then such a sentence is not true. This is why (3) is considered a case of mental confusion, if it is understood to represent the situation of (1) or (2). So it must be emphasized that whatever is generated is generated in the pre-existing context of a situation as viewed by the speaker. The speaker applies only those rules which refer to the given situation.

170. + Loce-Other Cae

The locative (Loce) and other case words are placed next. See -*day* in (34), which is the locative of time for *give.* This rule also places *Bengal* as the locative after the zero place of its verb *be* (see Rule 87). Note that in some model sentences, e.g., (30) there is no Loce, which means that the speaker may not have felt the presence of locative in his situation or, if it was felt, it was not considered necessary for, or essential to, the expression. It is possible to apply this rule optionally by placing the symbol (Opy) for optionality at the beginning. The only other case word is *telecommunication* of (40) as the Inl case.

171. Opy + Adb 'Time'

This rule optionally places an adverb of time here. See *now* in (37).

172. Sente Order ——173

This rule applies in terms of the order of sentences.

173. Opy + Sente$_1$ + Sente$_2$ + Sente$_3$...

The sequence of sentences is put in the order of the first sentence first, then the second, the third, and so on. This rule implies that the situation which was experienced first, occurs first as a sentence; then the second situation occurs next as the second sentence; and thus we have a whole discourse like (36i–36iii). Note the definition of sentence as given in Rule 134.1 It is clear now that a sentence may arouse a new situation also in the experience of the hearer, who in turn may become the speaker and change his or her experience into another sentence. Note that ' + ' places a sentence also.

174. Sente 'Contentive'-Sente 'Content' Order ——176

Here the order of contentive sentences, as in Rule 147, and of content sentences, as in 146, is described.

175. + Sente 'Contentive'

176. + Sente 'Content'

These two rules state that contentive sentences are placed first and content sentences next. Thus, in (40), *Now (you) send her the message by telecommunication* is a contentive sentence and, therefore, is placed before the content sentence *that Ray was an aggressor.*

In a detailed grammar there would be many other orders for these two types of sentences, which would be described within the domain of Rule 174. For example, in a sentence like *The message that Ray who kicked the bucket was an aggressor was sent by him to her,* the content sentence is placed not after the contentive sentence, but rather after the contentive word. There may be other such options.

177. Adje-Sped Word Order ——185

This rule is the same as Rule 47. Its domination goes through Rule 185.

178. + Prepon

The preposition is placed first. In (29) *by* was selected to occur with *boy* in accordance with Rule 143. Now Rule 178 places the preposition first.

179. *to* ÷ Date ÷ 165 → $\emptyset$

The preposition *to* of the dative of Rule 165 is replaced by zero. Rule 178 places the preposition *to* before *her* in (31). But in (34) this preposition is deleted before the dative *her,* because it is placed after the verb and before the object by Rule 165. This means that the sequence *That boy gives to her them* is not possible. Thus *to* will not be replaced by zero when dative occurs by Rule 168. In a detailed grammar, however, these rules will have to be modified.

180. + Arte, Pron Adje, *every*

The article (Arte) word, or the pronoun adjective (Pron Adje) word, or the adjective *every* is placed next. See *a* before *girl* and *the* before *boy* in the model sentences. Pronoun adjectives like *that* or *those* are also placed before their specified nouns by this rule. The adjective *every* is placed before *day* by this rule. Rule 180 lists three kinds of adjectives by means of commas. This means that only one kind is possible at a time. Thus, sequences like *that every day* or *that boy the a* cannot occur.

Examples (not included in our data) like *at which time* or *at what time,* containing relative or interrogative adjectives, are also within the domain of the Pron Adje of Rule 180.

181. + Other Adje

This is the same rule as 49. See *rough* of (35) as an example.

182. + Sped

This is Rule 50. See *forests* in (35) as the specified (Sped).

183. + Rele Pron ÷ Sped ——184

The relative pronoun (Rele Pron) of the specified noun of Rule 182 is placed next. In (40), *Ray* is the specified and his relative pronoun is *who.* Rule 183 places *who* after *Ray.* It is assumed here that a pronoun refers to a noun. That is, *who* refers to Ray in (40). So *who* is placed after *Ray.*

184. + Remaining Rele Sente

Then the remaining relative sentence (Rele Sente) is placed next. Thus, after *who* the remaining sentence which is relative is *kicked the bucket.* Rule 184 is within the domain of Rule 183.

Note that the content sentence *That Ray was an aggressor* has *Ray,* for which there is the relative pronoun in the sentence *who kicked the bucket.* Rules 183–184 insert the relative pronoun *who* along with the rest of the relative sentence after *Ray.* Thus, the total content sentence *That Ray was an aggressor* now turns out as *That Ray who kicked the bucket was an aggressor.*

Then there are other linear phonological changes which take place within or on the word boundary. These are called sandhi rules also, e.g., Rule 1. In our model sentences, for some speakers two consonants may be reduced to only one. This can be exemplified by *can* and *not,* which are placed next to each other by Rule 162.

185. $C_1C_1 \rightarrow C_1$

This rule states that a sequence of two identical consonants is replaced by only one of them. Thus the sequence *nn* in *cannot* is reduced to single *n.* Place the symbol Opy before this rule if it is optional.

Box F of Figure 1 implies that when a sentence is complete with all the words it is then pronounced by the speaker. This means that there must be pronunciation rules also. The sounds listed or shown with a concept are abstract impresions. That is, the sounds of *boy,* for example, are *b, ɔ,* and *y,* which are implied here by italicizing the word. What we have assumed is that when the speaker selects the concept *boy* he is aware of these three impressions, namely *b, ɔ,* and *y.* These impressions have to be activated by certain articulatory movements. Thus, we need the description, for example, of the sound impression *b* of *boy.* It would be described as 'bilabial voiced stop'. This is equal to a kind of instruction to articulate the sound symbol *b* by moving this or that part of the vocal tract in this or that manner. All the sounds are described in this way. Then there are some other phonetic components which are imposed upon the sounds according to the situation of a sentence. This is one reason for calling them 'suprasegmentals', since they are imposed upon a sound depending on the context and situation. For example, the pitch system, known as intonation, varies from sentence to sentence. The question intonation of (36i) might raise the relative pitch on the last vowel of *killer,* as opposed to the relative lower pitch on the same vowel of the same word in (36ii). Then, there is the difference of relative pause at the boundaries of various words. Pauses are also motivated by the situational experience. The pauses or junctures do not determine the word boundary. Evolutionarily, it is the other way around.

A detailed grammar should give rules of intonation, pauses, etc., and must associate them with some sort of sense that exists in the situation of the words and sentences. We cannot assume that sounds or pitches occur in some sort of structural blank spaces.

There is another question: Should we describe a sound's pronunciation in terms of the distinctive features proposed by Jakobson, Fant and Halle (1963) or in terms of articulatory components? We have indicated before that pronunciation means moving certain parts of the vocal tract in some manner in order to activate the abstract sound impressions like *p, b, t, d,* etc. If we are talking about vocal parts or manner, then it is implied that the actual basis for pronunciation must be articulatory or physiological.

This, however, does not mean that two sounds must not be distinguished minimally by a distinctive feature. In fact, this criterion is the main cause for considering two phones as distinct sounds. That is, *p* and *b* are different because of the minimal distinction of the absence or presence of 'voicing' respectively. I support such criterion because it does demonstrate that linearity is immaterial in the basic distinction of sounds. But the distinctive features proposed by Jakobson, Fant and Halle are mostly abstract. The sounds are already at the abstract level. It would be redundant to involve another set of features marked by abstractness, which has again a corresponding set of articulatory correlates. Articulatory means concrete pronunciation and that is what really takes place at the last stage of the sentence.

The pronunciation features of sounds are not central to language description. The central elements or units are the sounds. We have considered sounds as abstract impressions or sound images, of which the speaker is aware in the context of various concepts needed in the sentence. The child actually learns linguistic sound production by hearing. Hearing implies impressions that eventually motivate the intention of articulating a sound. The child does not know what vocal parts and manners are involved in the articulation of a sound. Even the adult speaker does not know this. That is, in reality the articulation of sounds is done impressionistically. We observe this behavior in music—another system of sounds. In natural music, e.g., folk singing, we can see how a child learns to articulate various pitches or tones impressionistically. An average musician is not aware of actual frequencies or vibrations of vocal cords, even though they are the physical or physiological reality underlying the production. (See more on this topic in Chandola 1977.) The point is that the impressionistic aspect of sounds transcends their articulatory aspect in importance. This can be shown by the following illustration.

The traditional complementary distribution principle can be

applied in the linear sense, which would go against the impressionistic criterion. Consider *h* and ŋ which would be allophones of one and the same phoneme. That is, *h* does not occur in the position where ŋ occurs. This is a linear distinction. But this does not reflect the actual phonetic awareness of the speaker. This can be tested impressionistically. Should we pronounce the *h* of *hot* as ŋ the word would be unrecognized with the meaning 'hot'. Similarly, pronounce the ŋ of wrong as *h* and the word will not be recognized as 'wrong'. This means that *h* and ŋ are distinct from each other. Nor can linearity be accepted as the basis for such distinctness. (See Chandola 1969 for more examples.) Our main reason for not using notions like phoneme, allophone, etc., is that these notions are based on complementary distribution, a principle which involves linearity for distinguishing one sound from another. However, complementary distribution such as found in the works of Bloch and Trager (1942), Pike (1947), Harris (1951), and others is useful for devising alphabets and for language decipherment.

We have stopped our description in this chapter without actual pronunciation rules of the sounds that occur in our model sentences. We have already stated that sounds are the real functional units of the phonological aspect of language description, not the features that are inherent or basic in a sound. But there would be many more non-phonological rules in a detailed description. We have seen how rules have to be modified or revised when more data is included. Even the limited data presented here needs more rules for complete explanation. But even such additional rules or explanation can be presented in the manner of the rules already given above. The next chapter will show how some of the rules given here reveal cause-and-effect relationships in the historical development of certain patterns in English.

VI

DIACHRONIC EVIDENCE

It was indicated in the first chapter that a natural description must reveal the evolutionary order of past linguistic events responsible for the present shape of a language. We will now evaluate our method of the preceding chapters in this light. This can be done by a comparison of OE (Old English) with NE (Modern English), which will show how our description enables us to see what is really lost and what preserved. For this purpose we will use the following OE examples as models. The abbreviations for OE nominal endings are N = nominative, G = genitive, D = dative, A = accusative, I = instrumental. Only selected forms will be cited here. The noun *stān* 'stone' is masculine, *giefu* 'gift' is feminine, and *hunta* 'hunter' is masculine. The OE adjective *blind* 'blind' is the indefinite type below. The pronominal forms in (43) stand for 'he, she, it', and 'this'. Forms of 'that' and 'stone' in (44) show agreement (vowel length omitted, e.g., *sē = se)*.

(41) *Singular:* N. stān, giefu, hunt-a; G. stān-es, gief-e, hunt-an; A. stān, gief-e, hunt-an; etc. *Plural:* N. stān-as, gief-a, hunt-an; G. stān-a, gief-a, hunt-ena, etc. (cited in Baugh 1935:67)

(42) *Masculine Singular:* N. blind-∅, G. blind-es, D. blind-um, A. blind-ne, I. blind-e. *Masculine Plural:* N. blind-e, G. blind-ra, D. blind-um, A. blind-e (cited in Stevick 1968:159)

(43) *Masculine Singular:* N. hē, þēs; G. his, þisses; D. him, þissum; A. hine, þisne, etc. *Feminine Singular:* N. hēo, þēos; A hīe, þas, etc. *Neuter Singular:* N. hit, þis, etc. *Common Plural:* N. hīe, þas; D. him, þissum, etc. (cited in Stevick 1968:146)

(44) *Singular:* N. se stan, A. þone stan, etc. *Plural:*N./A. þa stanas, etc. (cited in Traugott 1972:202)

In the following OE sentences used as models the transcription and translation is the same as that given in the source from which they are quoted. Sentences (45) and (46) make one continuous discourse:

(45) On þyssum ēalande cōm ūp se Godes þeow Augustinus and his gefēran; wæs hē fēowertiga sum. 'On this island came up the servant of God, Augustine and his companions; he was one of forty.'

(46) Nāmon hīe ēac swelce him wealhstodas of Francelande mid, swā him Sanctus Gregorius bebēad. 'Took they likewise with them interpreters from Frank-land, as them Saint Gregory bade.' (from Bede's *Ecclesiastical History* in Baugh 1935:74)

(47) he him hamweard ferde to his agnum rice. 'he him homeward went to his own kingdom = he went (betook) (himself) home to his own kingdom.' (from King Alfred's *Orosius* in Traugott 1972:89)

(48) 7 *his* (genitive, Patient) se cyning þær onfeng æt fulwhite. 'and him the king there received at the baptismal ceremony.' (from *Chronicle* in Traugott 1972:81)

(49) he þær beswicen weard from his agnum monnum (dative). 'he there betrayed was by his own men.' (*Orosius* in Traugott 1972:81)

(50) Persa cyning benom þone (accusative) *ealdormon* his shire. 'Persian's king deprived that chief of his shire.' (*Orosius* in Traugott 1972:80)

(51) ær þon hit þurh *ænne þeowne mon* (accusative) geypped weard. 'before it by a serving man revealed was.' (*Orosius* in Traugott 1972:80)

Let us discuss case. Case is not an inflection, as is very clear from the description given in Chapter V (see Rules 62 and 110). For example, *boy* in (29)–(34) is actor everywhere, but its inflections are not the same in all sentences. Inflections are ending suffixes; the actor *boy* occurs with prime in (32), but with second in (29). Similarly, *he* as actor in (33) has prime, but second in (30), which causes a stem change with *he* becoming *him*. (See Rules 111–118, 135.) In other words, one and the same case may be represented by different inflections in different sentences, or one and the same inflection may represent more than one kind of case. See (48) where *his* has a genitive ending (inflection), but is the object case of the activity represented by the word *onfeng* 'received', which could possibly have taken the accusative or dative ending, e.g., *him*. The word *he* in (49) does not represent the actor, yet has the nominative ending. Cases or their meanings are much more intrinsic and are universal, whereas languages differ in the inflections of nouns, etc. So terms like nominative, accusative, etc., must be understood as endings, not cases. In order to avoid confusion about dative it is better to write here 'dative case', as distinct from 'dative ending'. This is one reason why terms like 'prime, second, third, fourth' are better for ending classes. NE is considered to have lost the case system. This is a misunderstanding, caused by the fact that cases are confused with nominal inflections. Thus the situation underlying (1) has the subject case *boy*, object case *fruits* and locative case *day* for the verb *give*. These cases are universal in the sense that they refer to the items of the situation of (1) and potentially occur in any language, irrespective of time and place. What we can conclude is not that the OE case system collapsed in NE, but rather that NE has lost most of the inflections of OE nominals.

Most of the handbooks state that NE nouns have only two inflections—one the plural -*s* and the other the genitive -*s*. This misconception is rooted in several misleading approaches in modern linguistics. One is the notion of complementary distribution; another view is that meaning is either not relevant or, if it is, then only at a secondary level. If such views are taken seriously, the plural -*s* with nouns and the singular -*s* with present stems of verbs in the third person would have to be considered one and the same morpheme, since the two contexts of this -*s* are non-contrastive. Such a morphological description would blur not only the synchronic facts of NE, but also suppress the diachronic information otherwise preserved in NE. So we have not used the term or notion of morpheme. Instead, the term 'concept' has been used here as Sapir used it. Our approach becomes clear from Rules 119, 120, and 127, which posit three suffixes, each having the phonetic shape *s*. Now we can see that each *s* corresponds to separate sources diachronically. We have evidence that the function of the nominative ending in OE is that of prime in NE. The function of the OE accusative, dative, and instrumental endings is the same as that of second in NE. Thus we can generalize the diachronic evolution in the following rules:

186. OE Nominative Ending → NE prime
187. OE Accusative, Dative, Instrumental Endings → NE second
188. (OE Genitive Ending → NE genitive ending)

This evolution is further evidenced by the fact that NE has overt phonetic components, coming from some of the phonetic components of the corresponding OE endings. Thus the *s* of NE prime in the plural is from the *-as* of the OE nominative, e.g., NE *stones* and OE *st*ānas. The *s* of NE second plural is from the *-as* of the OE non-nominative plural ending, e.g., NE *stones* with second should be from OE accusative plural *st*ānas. The genitive is equally clear. Note that many OE nouns, *st*ān, *giefu, hunta,* etc., have the same forms in accusative plural as in nominative plural, yet no one states that the accusative plural is lost in OE. This is because the contrast can be clearly seen in other nominals, e.g., both singular and plural pronouns. Some OE nouns also have a phonetic contrast between nominative and accusative singular. The nouns *giefu* and *hunta* in (41) show this distinction. In other words, if some members do show some kind of overt phonetic contrast in the two forms, then we accept the two categories in the case of those forms which are identical in their phonetic shapes as well. This is the criterion adopted for OE and should be that used for NE too. NE pronouns do show contrastive forms in prime and second ending and, therefore, the same contrast must be accepted for nouns and adjectives, including the articles, since all pronouns, nouns, and adjectives are subclasses of the major class called nominals. Not to accept this principle of 'partial phonetic contrast' is not only to have double standards, but also suggests that English is a very illogical language. Thus, for example, Stevick has shown ∅ endings for OE adjectives in some forms as shown in (42). If we examine Proto-Germanic or even Proto-Indo-European (PIE) we see that those ∅ forms are justified. We can posit zeros in the prime and second endings of NE adjectives by contrasting them with NE pronouns and pronominal adjectives. Then we find that historically there were overt phonetic contrasts where we have zeros today. Compare, for instance, the OE nominative masculine singular *blind* with the corresponding Gothic form *blinds*, where *-s* of the ending is related to the P-Germanic nominative singular * *-a-z,* PIE * *-(o)-s* (Wright 1954:36, 85, 105).

What we observe here is that the zeros posited descriptively do not turn out to be arbitrary historically. Consider, for example, the infinitive suffix symbolized as nfnt. This suffix is replaced by zero (see Rule 130). The OE infinitive form of *cōm* of (45) is *cuman,* where *an* is the phonetic representation of the infinitive suffix. When we say that the infinitive suffix in NE is replaced by zero we imply that the infinitive suffix does exist, but it has no overt phonetic shape anymore. Here the intention is not to justify a zero form of the infinitive merely because we want to link it to the known fact that OE has an overt form of this suffix; rather it is strictly on descriptive grounds. It is the efficiency of the descriptive method which helps unfold this historical truth. Note that in the explanation of Rule 130 we had already said that descriptively we need to posit an infinitive suffix. To be consistent we have to assume that if some members of a symbol have an overt phonetic shape, then other members of that same symbol must also have a phonetic shape, although it may be zero.

This principle can be exemplified by adding changes like *fright:frighten, worse:worsen.* Here we see that nouns can be changed to verbs by adding a verbalizer suffix whose phonetic shape in these examples is *en.* Then there are examples like *stone:stone, blind:blind,* etc., where the first member of the pair is a noun, while the second is a verb. Thus we have sentences like *They stoned her* or *The dust blinded them.* Once we assume that verbalizer suffixes like *en* change some nouns to verbs, then we have to extend this analogy in order to change the noun *stone* to the verb *stone.* Thus, the verbalizer in the case of *stone* is represented by zero phonetic shape. We apply this principle consistently, irrespective of our knowledge of the historical development of verbalizers. What we want to emphasize here is that zeros cannot be posited arbitrarily at the descriptive level. These zeros eliminate the possibility of double standards.

The double standard policy is seen at various levels of linguistic description. We have shown in the fourth chapter how in other methods the principle of minimal distinction at a non-linear stage is acceptable for sounds (or phonemes) and concepts, whereas sentences are distinguished minimally from each other by linear means. The notion of case is another example. The strangest thing in this respect is that almost every linguist accepts, at some level, the notion of 'subject' and 'object'. Normally, a subject means the doer of an action or activity (verb). That is, a noun is being associated with a verb by means of some relation or function. This is also what is implied when we add more terms like 'locative', 'instrumental', 'dative', etc. A locative means the place where an action (verb) happens. An instrumental is that item which functions as a means of doing the action (verb). And so on. We notice a common pattern emerge here: nouns are related to verbs through certain functions. Such functions are covered by the term 'case'. That is, subject, object, locative, instrumental, etc., are the functions of nouns directly involved with an activity (verb). If we refuse to accept instrumental, locative, dative, etc., as cases in English, then we would be inconsistent, since we already accept terms like subject and object. Once we eliminate such inconsistency we find that many functions, suffixes, etc., really are not lost. Let us illustrate this point again with examples of endings.

Endings mark the word boundary in OE exactly the way they do in NE. This means Rules 103-105 are good at all stages of English. They are even valid for all other Indo-European languages. The endings relate one word with another by means of agreement or concord. The agreement behavior cannot be justified without positing three classes of nominal endings in NE. Rules 149-150 describe the NE agreement with the greatest simplicity. This simplicity is achieved through generalization. The optimum generalization is possible only when we base our description on the natural cause-and-effect principle. For example, we first apply Rules 111-118 which state the relationship between case and ending. Which case goes with which ending is detailed. Then 149 comes into play, which states that the case with prime and the ending of its verb agree in number. This description would fit the agreement of OE also. Similarly, 150 states the agreement between adjectives and the nominals they specify; this also would apply to OE. This is demonstrated in (47) by the agreement of *he* and the verb *ferde,* because *he* is a case occuring with the nominative (prime) ending. In (47) *he* is the subject case, but *he* in (49) is object case. Yet the verb agrees with it since it has the nominative (prime) ending. Compare the agreement of *agnum* 'own' with *monnum* 'men' in (49) and that of *ænne* 'an, a' with *mon* 'man'. Notice also that the indefinite article has the overt phonetic shape of the acusative ending in OE, whereas that shape is replaced by ꝺ in the corresponding *a* of NE, according to Rule 120. See (44) where third person pronominal adjectives and the noun specified by them are in agreement in terms of endings.

The many zero phonetic shapes or identical phonetic shapes of the NE endings seem to have a great effect on word order. For example, the most common pattern in NE is that the case which has prime occurs before the verb it is related to in statement-type sentences. The word *boy* in (32), like *he* in (33), is subject and has prime ending. The word *she* of (30) is the dative case, but has prime. The word *they* is object case in (31), but has prime. In simple words, we can generalize that a case with prime ending occurs before the verb, as was stated in 160. We do not see this kind of restriction in OE sentences. Compare the verbs *cōm* 'came' and *wæs* 'was' in (45), and *nāmon* 'took' in (46); they occur before their subjects, which are respectively *Augustinus* 'Augustine' and *he* 'he' in (45), and *hīē* 'they' in (46).

If a language has more inflections with overt differentiation in phonetic shape, it is theoretically possible to place a case before or after the verb and any case could appear after any other. See, for instance, the position of the object case *him* in (47) and *his* in (48). Thus in (47) we have the word order of subject + object + verb..., whereas in (48) we have the word order of object + subject + ...verb.... The objects are clearly marked by their different phonetic shapes due to their respective endings. In (45) the subjects occur after the verbs yielding the word order of verb + subject.... Here also the phonetic shape of the subjects with their nominative endings distinctly mark the subject. The word *on* and the dative endings of þyssum 'this' and *ēalande* will serve the function of indicating the locative case of *ēalande* 'island', no matter where they are placed in (45). Wherever the word *ēalande* is placed, the coocurrent words *on* and *þyssum* will be placed before it, just as in Rules 178-182.

Not only smaller units like inflections influence word order, but even much smaller units which compose the inflections affect the possibilities of the forthcoming word order. If more phonetic contrasts characterize the various inflections, the word order is going to be more flexible and vice versa. If so, then it is obligatory to apply the rules involving inflections before we apply the word order rules. Consider Rule 160. This rule places a case with prime before an auxiliary or main verb (see Rules 161 and 163). Rule 160 can apply only when 113 and 116 have been taken care of. Rules 119-120 indicate that there are not that many overt phonetic contrasts in the endings. The reaction to this is that a more rigid word order had to develop in NE. In other words, a case word with prime ending occurs with little or no exception before the verb word in a statement-type sentence. Thus in the application of these rules the evolutionary reason for placing a particular word before another word is implied.

Unfortunately, in the available descriptions of English we do not find explanations for such an action-reaction chain, starting from the smaller units and going up to the larger ones. Consider the TG approach. It starts with the largest unit and decomposes it into smaller units in a very arbitrary manner, as we saw in Rules 2-4. In (1) a rule like NP + VP is supposed to place the phrase *the boy* before the verb phrase *gives*. At least two more rules are needed to take care of types like (29) and (30): one rule to place the object NP *fruits* before the verbs *are given* in the passive sentence (29) and another to place *she*, as in (30), before *is given*. Thus the achievement of Rule 160 is described by TG in at least three rules, with many more symbols per rule, as well as repetition of the same symbols on both sides of the arrow.

The worst implication of such TG rules is that linearity of phrases is not affected by the endings. It suggests that the endings are placed *after* the phrases are positioned in a linear order. The result is that the rules of agreement in TG become very complex. We have observed in OE that case words can be placed more freely because of the overt phonetic differentiation among the endings. This happens in other old Indo-

European languages too. TG rules would imply that those Indo-European speakers used linearity first to indicate functions like subject, object, etc., and after their linearization they also attached endings to indicate the same functions. That is, those speakers used two systems to denote one and the same function. Our question is: Does the human brain really allow for such inefficiency? The TG rules, intentionally or unintentionally, have this as their absurd implication—that in some languages the mental processes involve great waste, whereas in others such waste does not occur. The fact is that linearity is a secondary development. It arises out of the phonetic nature of the concepts. Meaning, functions, or relations of situational items exist before the decisions on their linearity are made.

The linear approaches, including TG, fail to totally reveal the reasoning for the subject of (32), the object of (29), and the dative of (30) occupying one and the same linear position in NE, when each of them could have occupied many more positions in OE. Simple listing of positions under the name of a structure or transformation does not explain the real descriptive reasons. A formation, after all, is the result of certain actions and reactions that took place earlier. A powerful description is capable of revealing not only the present reality, but also the background that caused such a reality. Things cannot hapen in a vacuum. To count things and place them with a structural title, in an arbitrary order in empty spaces, is merely plain reporting, devoid of subtle explanation. To state that an apple falls from a tree onto the ground is plain reporting. But if we involve the phenomenon of gravity as a cause for the falling, then we are providing a subtle explanation. The subtle explanatory power of the description lies in unfolding the causes and effects that made and placed those things in the way they are. Mathematical niceties are fine only if they help explain such an evolutionary or causal development. So far all methods fall short of this goal. It is hoped that linguists will use not only mathematics, but other disciplines as well to achieve this goal. But above all, linguistic formation is best understood in its own background and setting, using its own terms. There are so many languages whose history, unlike that of Hindi or English, is not at all documented. And then there

VII

FINAL STATEMENT

A Sentence is a natural product. Natural growth involves various elements in an environment which gradually evolve larger or higher elements. Conventional language descriptions all have some sort of compartmental regimentation with phonology, morphophonemics, morphology, syntax, semantics and many more, such as suggested by Lamb (1966). These compartments may be considered useful in some ways e.g., for pedagogical convenience; but the evolution of a sentence cannot be explained in any hierarchical order of these compartments. In current approaches, much emphasis is given to syntactic and semantic explanations. We cannot, however, start the evolution of sentences with the symbol S (Sentence) and then decompose it into smaller constitituents, like Noun Phrase, Verb Phrase, etc. The symbol S is higher than its constituent parts. It is impossible for a larger symbol to exist before its constituent symbols.

One cannot start with phonetic or phonological units, in the sense that they are some kind of smallest elements. Evolutionarily, the production of sounds is for the purpose of expressing the meaning of a concept. This purpose has to occur before its expression. The meaning or semantic components, then, seem to be the starting point of a sentence. But the purpose of a concept is to denote some item of a situation. The notion that concepts are selected because of the compatibility of their semantic features does not explain why the speaker selects a limited number of concepts in a given sentence.

Recent lexical theories are attempting to describe concepts with their limited semantic as well as syntactic features. For examples of how some of these theories work, see Jackendoff (1975). We must realize that concepts are pontentially unlimited, unless a language dies or has very few speakers left. It is true that an individual has a limited vocabulary. But it is also true that a speaker can improvise the existing conceptual material according to the realistic or imaginative aspects of a situation. It is not clear from such lexical descriptions of concepts why and in what order those features take place. A lexicalist hypothesis cannot account for the improvisational and creative formation and combination of concepts in the absence of certain general rules.

In the sense of descriptive evolution, the experience of situational items and their relations must exist *before* a speaker decides to select matching concepts. In other words, such matching is possible only after an activity, its cases, and various specifiers of that activity, etc., are analyzed as such by the psychological potential with which a speaker is endowed naturally. It is true that concepts, except new ones, are available to the speaker even before the experience of a situation. But in a synchronic sense we must assume that concepts are created for the purpose of items. The concepts are recreated or reproduced every time they are selected to match an item. Without the existence of items and their interrelationships, it would be impossible to activate any concept. In the process of reproduction it is not always possible to preserve all of their semantic and phonetic components intact; this explains one of the basic underlying causes of language change.

The selection of concepts implies that they must be linearized, since their composition also contains sound impressions. That is, the sounds have to be represented as one after another, because of the simple fact that a speaker can produce only one sound at a time. This is another reason for not accepting lexical entries or concepts as the domain where sentential elements are first evolved, since the items referred to by the concepts are not basically viewed by the speaker in any tangible order. The items exist in a situation simultaneously. This is not to say that one activity, its cases, specifiers, etc., cannot be followed by another activity, its cases and specifiers. Rather what is being emphasized here is that no activity with its cases can be said to display any order of time and space at the situational level. The timing and spacing which we observe in the end is due to the fact that the speaker ultimately has to pronounce the situation in the form of a sentence. Thus, we cannot consider the timing and spacing as the starting point of the evolutionary process of a sentence. The linear approaches are misleading when they explain the evolution of the so-called surface structures from the deep structures on the basis of such timing and spacing.

The notion of conceptual compatibility, however, does work. But it works because that is what the speaker views in his situation. This compatibility changes according to the view taken by the speaker and this change may not match the features listed by the analyst. In our approach, Rule 5 types are formulated to take care of such problems.

Moreover, lexical theories cannot account for the mental confusion of the speaker. A sentence may be well-formed because it displays perfect compatibility among all the concepts, yet it does not represent the underlying situation. This fact cannot be brought out by any current linguistic theory and method. This means that a situational view of language is necessary. Figure 1 suggests the evolution of a situation into a sentence. Sentences (1) and (2) are well-formed because they begin with Box A and go through Box F. Sentence (3) would be treated as well-formed in all other linguistic theories and methods. But we do not consider (3) well-formed at all. The reason is that the analysis which the speaker's mind or brain does of the situation of sentence (1) is not expressed by sentence (3). We have said before that the situational analysis is converted into a sentence through certain mental processes. The situational understanding of the speaker starts this chain of processes underlying a given sentence. The theory and method of language description must indicate this chain as far as possible. It is possible to account for many language disorders if we study this chain. Sentence (3) is only an example of just such a disorder.

The failure of sentence (3) as a representative of the situation of (1) implies many things. One, for example, is that form does not exist primarily for its own sake. The other is that mere psycho-physiological or acoustic reality of sounds and their sequences is not the fundamental source of a sentence, even if such sequences represent all possible compatible concepts or words. Sentence, at its most primitive source, is neither concepts nor their linearity, but pure situational items and their interrelationships. Any creature with a brain must be competent to analyze a situation which involves some items and their interrelationships, otherwise it simply could not react to anything in an environment. Because of this common potential, humans can even establish some sort of primitive communication with animals. (See for example, Chandola 1963.)

Therefore, it is of immense importance that a natural description display the evolutionary track through which the smaller elements were assembled and processed into higher elements. A grammar must apply its rules with the basic assumption that rules first refer to the items and their mutual relations or functions, while implying the selection of the corresponding concepts. Linearization rules must follow. And every rule must imply the cause-and-effect chain underlying a formation.

The preceding chapters elaborated these points. Our description of certain given English sentences demonstrated that our method has rules which apply with a set of conditions and assumptions. The rules picture mental processes as a system which produces a sentence with optimum generalization, involving minimum repetition of a rule or symbols. This is possible only when the rules capture the root cause of an effect at the right point in the evolutionary track. This track is not revealed by means of the traditional compartments, hence they must be disregarded. It is essential to disregard them because clear demarcation of these compartmental boundaries is impossible.

In this respect even the newer compartments, such as used in the TG models, have to be disregarded. We have shown earlier how the PS rules blur the evolutionary process. One classic case is that TG rules like 2–4 imply that selection and linearity of such phrases as NP, Aux, VP, etc., are simultaneous. Consider the sentence (6) of Sanskrit. If we have a PS rule like Rule 2 for Sanskrit, then it means that NP_1 implies the function of subject as we see in the word *bālakaḥ* of (6). Suppose the base *bālaka* 'boy' is assumed here as the NP_1, instead of the whole word *bālakaḥ*. Rule 2, however, does not state what ending or inflection NP_1 would take. Eventually, there has to be a TG rule which will attach the phonetic form of the nominative inflection or ending, namely *h*, to the base or stem *bālaka*. The nominative ending here is for the purpose of subject. The question is this: Why does the brain have to employ two systems—phrase order and inflectional suffixes —to indicate one and the same function, namely the function of subject, when one is enough? If we assume that a normal human brain operates with optimum efficiency in sentence formation, then TG rules fail to characterize such an efficency.

It could be argued that the subject NP has to occur somewhere in (6), even if the inflectional suffixes are attached before the application of Rules like 2–4. Such an argument, however, is needless, if we realize that the placement or linearity of words is necessitated primarily because the sounds of concepts can be produced only one after another. Thus, the very nature of such sound production makes word order inevitable in every language. In some languages the functional load is heavier on the word order, whereas in others it is very low. For instance, there would be relatively fewer word order rules in OE compared to NE. The reason is that OE has more word endings than NE, as shown in Chapter VI. Here we observe that word·endings and word order display a cause-and-effect relationship. We can understand the functional load of word order only after we have understood the nature of word formation in a language. On the basis of the word forms it is possible to predict whether a language will have relatively flexible or rigid word order. We can, for example, predict that if the word forms do not contain any overt elements within themselves to indicate functions like subject, object, etc., then the order of the word forms will indicate such functions. Linguistic descriptions which start the syntactic description with phrase-structure rules cannot explain why certain constituents of those phrases can exchange positions quite freely in some languages, while in others exchange is not so free. If a phrase oriented approach, such as TG, had followed natural order of formation, then there would have been no need for it to resort to such arbitrariness. That is, by accepting the fact that larger elements react because of smaller elements, there would not have been any need for such compartments as base component and transformational component. On the surface it might seem that larger elements affect the smaller elements; but a deeper study shows that the ultimate cause for such effects is to be found in the smaller elements and in their interaction within a larger element. Breaking a sentence into 'phrases' may be useful only in a non-technical sense, e.g., in pedagogical contexts (Chandola 1970).

We have pointed out previously that concepts are reactivated or recreated every time they are selected from a list (dictionary or lexicon) and then linearized. This implies that formally language is constantly changing. Evolution refers to synchronic formation as well as to diachronic development. A powerful grammar implies by its very rules that the existing formal shape of linguistic units is the result of certain historical developments. These changes coming from the past of the language are reflected in the order of rule application.

There is then the whole primitive past of human evolution. How humans evolved language before they could manipulate the vocal tract for linguistic sound production is also reflected in the rule operation order. Like animals, humans must have had the ability to recognize items, however primitive they may have been, in the situations surrounding them. It is improbable that they recognized those items irrespective of any context. They must have seen those items related to each other, as well as to themselves. Those relations or functions are what we call activity, cases, specifiers, etc. Then the items they experienced gradually took the form of concepts, which they eventually began to linearize for the same reasons as mentioned above. Thus, it must be accepted that concepts or any other kind of grouping came much later in the history of language evolution. Even today humans have not been able to conceptualize everything they see or feel in their situations. This is one reason why existing concepts have to be improvised. Such an improvisation may gradually become permanent. In this way, new meanings can be added to the already existing list of a concept's meanings. Also the old meanings of that concept can be replaced wholly or partially by new meanings. Such changes may even be followed by changes in the phonetic components of that concept. Thus, the process of forming concepts will continue as long as humans retain the use of language.

It is interesting to note that, in a way, the entire past of human linguistic development is repeated in every speaker's life. The infant, it seems, is aware of his most primitive situations surrounding him and can observe or impose relations among the items of those situations, even before the acquisition of concepts. That is, a child's conceptualization of items must follow his understanding of the items and their relations in one or more situations. The meaning of the concept is followed by the association of its sounds. The child's ability to select concepts according to a given situation must precede the ability to linearize them in a given order. Thus, Figure 1 implies the process through which even a child evolves his sentences. And thus we can conclude by saying that history really does repeat itself.

EXPLANATION OF SYMBOLS AND SIGNS

For the sake of consistency and ease of predictability, the symbols used in the rules employ the following principles. A symbol may appear with its complete spelling, e.g., 'Actor', 'Item', 'prime' 'second', etc.; however, most of the symbols are abbreviated. The abbreviation system used is as follows: (1) Use only the first letter, e.g., M for 'masculine'. (2) Use the first (one or more successive) and last letters, e.g., Arte for 'article', where the first three letters 'a', 'r', and 't' are the first letters in succession and 'e' is the last. The italicized forms (underscored in typing) imply the phonetic representation in sounds. Roman numerals have been used for 'person', e.g., III means 'third person'. Sentence numbers appear in parentheses; rule numbers are without parentheses. The abbreviated symbols are listed below:

List of Symbols

Alphabetic Symbol	Full form	Alphabetic Symbol	Full form
Acy	activity	Date	dative
Adb	adverb	Dee	declinable
Adje	adjective	Devel	deverbal
Arte	article	Dit	direct
Auxy	auxiliary	Else	elsewhere
Bac	basic	Endoc	endocentric
Bae	base	Eng	ending
C	consonant	Equip	equimembership
Cae	case	F	feminine
Come	complete	Fine	finite
Compd	compound	Indee	indeclinable
Conct	concept	Inflen	inflection
Confe	confirmative	Inl	instrumental
Conjun	conjunction	Loce	locative
Cooct	co-occurrent	M	masculine

Alphabetic Symbol	Full form	Alphabetic Symbol	Full form
Mol	modificational	Ret	recipient
mprt	mprt	Sente	sentence
	'Imperative...'	Sir	singular
Nege	negative	Sped	specified
nfnt	infinitive	Sper	specifier
Nol	nominal	Subt	subject
Obt	object	Sux	suffix
Oby	obligatory	Tee	tense
Opy	optionally	Tre	transitive
Parte	participle	Ulte	ultimate
Partit	participant	V	vowel
Pase	passive	Vb	verb
Pl	plural	Vel	verbal
Prede	predicate		
Prepon	preposition		
Promit	prominent		
Pron	pronoun		
prt	prt 'Present...'		
pst	pst 'Past...'	*Roman*	
Pure	purposive	*Numeral*	*Full form*
Q	question	III	'third person'
Rece	receptive		
Refe	reference		
Rele	relative		

Below the list of signs is given. The rule number in parentheses at the end refers to one of the places where its explanation and/or example can be found.

List of Signs

Sign		Explanation
=	(the equal sign)	'is' (Rule 18)
≠	(the equal sign crossed with a slant bar)	'is not' (Rule 71)
:	(colon)	'occurs with' (Rule 8)
::	(double colons)	'agrees with' (Rule 35)
→	(arrow)	'is replaced by' (Rule 1)

⇸ (arrow crossed with a slant bar)	'is not replaced by' (Rule 153)
(((left parenthesis sign duplicated)	'with, containing' (Rule 72)
⫫ (left parenthesis sign duplicated and crossed with a slant bar)	'without' (Rule 109)
((left parenthesis sign)	'before' (Rule 132)
) (right parenthesis sign)	'after' (Rule 37)
÷ (division sign)	'of' (Rule 7.1)
× (multiplication sign)	'is compounded with' (Rule 90.1)
⇔ (equivalent sign)	'is like' (Rule 20)
+ (plus sign)	'linear instruction for words and sentences, e.g. 'Place now' (Rule 9)
—— (dash)	'linear instruction for concepts' (Rule 16)
- (hyphen)	'and' (Rule 47)
/ (slant bar)	'or' (Rule 34)

A comma sign ',' is used to list the two symbols on its two sides without any order (Rule 54.1). The semi-colon ';' indicates the progressive order from left to right between the symbols (Rule 53). The double slant bars '//' enclose a prose explanation (Rule 151). Three dots '...' indicate that there may be more symbols of the same class (Rule 54.1). Any symbol can be negated by crossing it with a slant bar, e.g., ':̸' meaning 'does not occur' is the opposite of the colon sign ':' which means 'occurs with'. Sometimes the pronunciation is given in brackets, e.g. [sʌn] in sentences (25)-(27). The symbol with an asterisk sign is considered 'inactive basically' (Rule 94). The sign '↔' is the plus sign with two arrow heads and it will be explained in Appendix B.

APPENDIX B

RULE EXPLANATION

For the order of rule application a system of numbering is most efficient. Here are a few examples. Some rules appear with a whole number and some with a whole number plus a decimal point. Such Rules as 51, 52, 71, 72, 85, 86, 119, 120, 164, 169, etc., are examples of the former type, wheareas Rules 54, 54.1, 60, 60.1, 64, 64.1, 73, 73.1, etc., are examples of the latter type. The explanation of a whole number plus a decimal point is given in the description of Rules 54, 54.1. The domain of a rule is indicated by placing to the right the number of the last rule which falls within such a domain: e.g., the domain of Rule 15 goes through Rule 32, which is indicated by the number 32 placed at the end of Rule 15. Another example of this convention and its explanation is given by Rule 52. The numbers imply progressive application of rules as explained in Rule 51. There will be conflicts in straight progressive application. However, such conflicts are easily resolved by a few conventions which are explained in the description of Rule 53.

A rule which follows another rule may have some symbols missing. In such a case, the symbols are provided from the immediately preceding rule. This device saves symbols and is explained in Rule 29. The conditional rule also applies to the immediately preceding rule, e.g., 82 applies to 81.

There is only one linear sign which has not been used in our rules. This is the plus sign with two horizontal arrow heads written as '←⊦→'. Below we show its use. But first consider these Hindi sentences:

(52) *bāghinē bāghaũ ko dekheṅgī.*
tigresses tigers PP will-see
'The tigeresses will see the tigers.'

where *ko* is the postposition (PP) as marker of the object. The word order in (52) is the most frequent, but there are other orders also, e.g.:

(53) *bāghaū ko bāghinē dekheṅgī.*
(54) *bāghinē dekheṅgī bāghaū ko.*
(55) *dekheṅgī bāghinē bāghaū ko.*
The meaning of (53)–(55) will be the same in English as that of (52). What we observe in Hindi is that the case words and verb words can occur or be placed in any order. Unlike English, the load of indicating case functions like subject, object, etc., is not put on the Hindi word order. This is because the word endings in Hindi are not only more in number, but also more diverse in overt phonetic representation than in English. Nonetheless, there will be case rules for Hindi in the manner of Rules 62–67. After applying case rules there will be ending rules, like 110–129. There may be other rules between the case rules and ending rules, but not word order rules. The word rules will apply, just as in English, only after all the word formation rules have been applied. Then the word order rules will apply in the manner of Rule 155. The only difference between the English and Hindi word order will be that of number. For example, consider the corresponding English sentence:

(56) *The tigresses will see the tigers.*

This English sentence will need at least these word order rules from Chapter V: 160 for *tigresses,* 161 for *will,* 163 for *see,* 166 for *tigers,* and 180 for *the.* Hindi, on the other hand, will have the following word order rule in place of 160:
189. ↔ Cae-Vb
This rule means 'Place freelẏ the case words and verb words'. The hyphen between Cae and Vb means 'and'; it is not a linearity sign. The ↔ sign places all the case words and verb words in all possible orders, as we see in the Hindi sentences (52)–(55). A rule is then needed to place the postposition *ko* after the object case word; it will be similar to 178 but in reverse order, because *ko* is a postposition (not a preposition) which is placed after the specified noun word, like that of Rule 182. This means that exceptions to a general rule, like 18y, can be taken care of later. Thus, where English will need at least three rules—one for subject, one for object, one for the verb—Hindi will need only one rule. On the other hand, Hindi will need more rules for word endings. Thus, there will be a proportionate balance of rules in any two languages in question.

This balance can be seen only in evolutionary terms. We can see, for instance, why Hindi needs fewer word order rules than English. However, English has fewer ending rules, while Hindi has more. It should not be construed here that word endings are the only factors causing the differences in the word order. There may be other overt markers in other languages for this purpose. The point is that the evolutionary scheme reveals the cause-and-effect chain by considering the formation of words first and their order later.

Moreover, Rule 189 eliminates the need of arbitrary constituent grouping and ordering. The operational waste which is inherent in TG rules is also eliminated by evolutionary rules. That is, if the object case (NP_2) is considered as part of VP in a TG rule like 3, then it is obvious that the order of (53) and (55) will have to be considered as transforms of either (52) or (54): e.g., NP_1 + NP_2 + V of (52) →NP_2 + NP_1 + V of (53). Notice here that the same symbols are repeated in this T rule. In fact, the Hindi sentence may have many other case words where more symbols will have to be repeated in the T rules. Not only case words or verb words can be moved here and there, but adjectives and adverbs also. Those who consider adjectives, for example, as a constituent of verb phrase, will face the same problems as, for example, are seen in considering NP_2 (object) as part of VP.

Thus, the system of TG involves here two operational wastes. One, the system has to pass through the base of (52) if it is to produce the transform as (53) or (55). The other, that if NP_1 and NP_2 positionally imply their functions, then the need for endings like $\tilde{e}$, $\tilde{au}$ or the PP *ko*, etc., of (52)–(55) seems to be superfluous in the TG description. It is totally unacceptable that an efficient production system will operate through a longer route, employing more stages of evolution for one and the same purpose, when it has the choice of a shorter route with minimum redundancy, plus the advantage of evolutionary explanation.

As a note, it may be argued here that rules like 2–4 can be presented with unordered constituents, or unconcatenated phrases, to account for sentence types like (52)–(55). For instance, Rule 2 can appear as S→NP, VP and Rule 3 as VP→ NP, V, where the phrases on the two sides of a comma occur freely.

Thus NP, VP means we can have NP_1 + VP as well as VP + NP_1 order. Similarly, NP, V means the order NP_2 + V as well as the order V + NP_2. But only a T rule can move NP_1 between NP_2 and V. Even if all or some PS rules are assumed to have totally unordered phrases, there will still be need for T rules in the TG method for various other types of syntactic changes. A T rule means duplication and repetition on both sides of the arrow. But in the integrated word order rules, such as 156–184, the proper reasons for a change can be observed. For instance, the change in the order of subject and object in the English passive can be justified only when various changes in the endings of the subject and object are accounted for. In Hindi the passive has the same relatively freer order as in the active sentences (52)–(55). Such a freer order suggests that the positions of cases are not as significant in Hindi as in English. Rules like 189 also suggest that some sort of order of words is otherwise inevitable, since sounds can occur only sequentially.

APPENDIX C

DESCRIPTION ORDER

We have already stated before that rules assemble concepts only when the itemic functions or situational sense of the items are known. Concepts are then assembled into words and words into sentences. The rules, therefore, apply in an order which explains how smaller elements develop larger elements. But besides rule order we can see the rules of Chapter V in terms of topics and their order. The topics, too, are arranged to reflect the evolutionary scheme. Thus, the topic of how items are understood in terms of various general concept categories is described in Rules 54-67. How concepts are associated with other concepts is described in Rules 68-139; how words are associated with words is described in Rules 140-184. Phonological changes, e.g., in stems, concepts or words, are automatically described in their respective levels. For example, Rules 135-139 deal with stem changes and are given within the description of concepts. On the other hand, the sandhi rules, which are due to the placement of words, should be given after the word order topic is complete. There may be sandhi rules that operate between concepts and they, therefore, belong to the topic of concepts (just after Rules 139). There may be rules which apply to concepts as well as to words; such rules should be given after all necessary rules about concepts and words are completed: e.g., the sandhi rule of 185 may apply on the boundary (sandhi) of concepts, as well as of words. This means that the 185 type topic should appear after all linear rules of concepts and words are finished.

There are, however, some general topics which can occur anywhere, e.g., definitions and conventions. To understand the application procedure of rules, it is better to state the conventions in the beginning, as was done in Rules 51-53. The definitions can also be given as they are needed, e.g., the definition of words in Rules 103-105, or the definition of sentence in Rule

134. Here, however, we should add that, to some extent, there is flexibility in the order of topics within the respective levels of concepts, words and sentences. For instance, the compound rules (90–98) can be discribed before the idioms (Rules 99–102), or Rules 135–139 (stem changes) can be given before inflections (110–131), and so on. Nonetheless, the conventions still operate in terms of conditioned order.

Partial flexibility in the order of topics suggests the existence of some freedom in the decision-making process of a speaker's psychological potential, which here we have roughly called the mind. There may be, however, a definite order determined by factors in either a speaker's attitude towards the situation, or in the brain mechanism itself, or in both, or perhaps elsewhere. This uncertainity stems partly from the fact that, as stated in Chapter II, we are unable to observe the order of priorities in such mental decisions. Consider a sentence like *Yesterday he killed that tiger in that boathouse instantly.* It is impossible to be certain whether the brain first decided upon the formation of *killed* or *yesterday, of instantly* or *boathouse,* etc. There are two occurrences of *that* in this sentence and we cannot be sure if they are picked up and distributed simultaneously. Similarly, we cannot definitely demonstrate that in sentence (32) the stem change from the base *he* to *her* took place before the stem change from the base *he* to *them* (it is so complex that even the adjective *that* of Rule 136 could be considered as an alternant stem of *he* of Rule 135). What we would like to know is whether the third person pronoun base (presented as *he* on the left side of the arrow in Rule 135) is the reference point or stage at which the alternants, like *he, they, her,* etc. (presented on the right side of the arrow in Rule 135) are picked up. If so, then the decision to pick up the third person pronoun base must be taken before one of the alternants (including *he*) is picked up.

It cannot be maintained that words are assembled in the order they are spoken in a sentence. The spoken order is dependent on linear order, which is in turn dependent on other non-linear relations or functions, as well as on the nature of sounds, as has been stated before. We cannot even assume that the priority of order of words reflects 'emphasis'. The same emphasis, if there is any, on *every day* of (33) can be placed on the *every day* of (34) by other means, e.g., by intonational changes.

Questions about the order of topics or the priorities of formations within one and the same level may some day be answered by further research in psycholinguistics or neurolinguistics. Whether or not these questions are answered, we have to assume that concepts cannot be activated without their association with the pre-existing situational sense and functions of the items as viewed by the speaker. Such an activation means their selection and linearity leading to word formation and eventually to the largest unit, which we call sentence. The formation of all these units and their linearization will still take place in terms of conventions, like the ones mentioned by Rules 51–53. These conventions implicitly seek the progressive application of rules with the least possibility of conflict, repetition, or double processing, for one and the same purpose. In view of such operational efficiency, certain topics precede certain other topics. For example, the topic of case precedes the topic of affixation and the topic of word order is given after the topic of word endings. Besides, there are also strong evolutionary reasons for such an order, as already stated. We do not know exactly how the brain or mental processes work out the details of formations. But it seems logical to assume that formations must take place most efficiently and this can happen only through the cause-and-effect principle, without which evolution cannot be explained.

APPENDIX D

APPLICATION OF TERMS AND RULES TO A SAMPLE SENTENCE

Let us consider (36i) as the sample sentence here. We assume that the speaker has the following items in his underlying situation: The main activity is 'be'. The actor related to this activity of 'being' is 'Ray'. We may not be able to exactly define here terms like 'activity', 'actor', 'verb', 'subject', etc., but the fact is that the speaker analyzes, knows or feels that 'Ray' is related to 'be', in the same way that any other actor is to its activity. Thus, a definition term is only symbolic, one which can always be replaced by any other, better term. For example, one may want to use the term 'agent' instead of 'actor'. The effect is still the same. That is, 'Ray' is to 'be' in (36i) what, for instance, 'boy' is to 'give' in (34). Here 'Ray' and 'boy' have one and the same function or relation to the main finite verbs, no matter how or what we designate, term or even rename that function. However, some designating does have to be given, mainly for two purposes: to account symbolically for the understanding of the speaker and to formulate rules.

Note that the understanding or analysis of a situation by the speaker does not necessarily match the factual truth of that situation. Consider *ghar* 'house' and *ā* 'come' in the following Hindi sentence:

(57) *śīlā kā ghar pās ā rahā hai.*
    Shiela of house close come-ing is
    'Shiela's house is coming close.'

Here one may question whether an inanimate item like *ghar* 'house' can really function as the subject of the motion verb *ā* 'come' in a factual situation. We have clearly intimated previously that such a case notion, such as that proposed by Fillmore (1968), is not pragmatic. What we do know is that in Hindi-speaking society and culture, sentences of the (57) type are as frequent as the following:

(58) *śīlā pās ā rahī hai.*

Shiela close come-ing is
'Shiela is coming close.'

Here it becomes very explicit that the verb in (57) agrees with its subject *ghar* (masculine singular) for the same reason it does with *śīlā* (feminine singular) in (58). Thus, the universality of case relations cannot be based on the factual behavior of the items of a situation, but rather must be based upon the attitudes or view taken by the speaker toward those items and their relationships. We canot posit as universal that an animate item alone can be the agent or subject; the universal must rather be worded, for formal purposes, as 'any item that is viewed as an actor or agent is renamed the subject'. The case meaning, or the situational sense it refers to, is universal, but not necessarily its formal delivery or expression. Not only may two languages differ in the formal expression of one and the same sense of a case, but the same case may be delivered, or overtly expressed, in more than one way in the same language. Why the speaker views his world thusly, however, is beyond the scope of linguistic description.

So 'Ray' and 'be' in (36i) are viewed with the relationship of actor and activity, implied by rules like 67, 67.1, and 57, 57.1. An item representing the party which 'kills tiger' is viewed as the predicate nominal (tiger killer); then the corresponding lexical items like *Ray, be, a, kill,* and *tiger* are selected. 'Ray' is felt as one person, thus the nominal stem *Ray* as base (Rules 70, 70.1 and 107) selects the suffix prime ending. The possibility of second ending is eliminated by Rules 111–112. The prime ending is placed after *Ray* by the linear rule 69; it must apply after selectional rules like 111 and 112 via the convention of Rule 53. The prime ending is phonetically zero by Rule 119.

The finite verb *be* selects a tense ending by Rule 109. Here this tense ending is prt because of the 'present' sense (Rule 122). Rule 69 applies immediately after this selectional rule does, again by the convention of Rule 53, placing prt after *be.* The prt suffix is first phonetically *s* via Rule 127 and then *z* via Rule 131. The stem of *be* is *i* according to Rule 139. One might argue that Rule 149 should apply prior to rules like 127, 131, etc., because the phonetic form of tense ending can only be determined after the agreement rule has applied. There are two ways to resolve this issue. One is to introduce Rule 149 before

Rule 127. The other is to admit that there is no real conflict between 127 and 149, since the phonetic shape is only going to be determined when Rule 149 is reached. That is, the possibility of other phonetic shapes, namely zero, for prt will be ruled out the moment we apply Rule 149. Thus, the selection of 127 is possible only after the application of Rule 149, because 127 does not tell us what number and person the prt ending would have in the case of *be* here.

Another aspect of this question is whether a child learns agreement before or after the acquisition of some endings. That is, the child may have first selected endings which he readjusts after becoming aware of the need for agreement. Can the order of rules here be said to reflect this early behavior—behavior which eventually becomes firm? This again leads to the problem of priorities discussed in Chapter II.

The verb stem *kill* selects the suffix concept *er* by Rule 78. Then *er* is placed after *kill* (Rules 69 and 53). The formation *killer* is a base according to Rule 72. Rule 92 refers to the compounding relationship of the object 'tiger' with its activity 'kill'. In this compound *tiger* is the one base (Bae_1) which is compounded with another base (Bae_2), namely *killer* (see Rules 90, 90.1) Rule 97 designates Bae_2 as Promit, so that Rule 98 places *tiger* first and *killer* next. Then the inflectional ending is selected for *killer*, not for *tiger*, via Rule 108, which is under the domain of Rule 107. Here we again have the issue of whether the agreement rule (150) should be applied before or after the ending rules (111, 112 and 119). This issue can also be resolved in exactly the way shown above, in the case of Rule 149 versus Rules 127 and 131. Incidentally, Rules 111, 112 and 150 apply to *a* also.

It should be emphasized again that selection and linearity cannot be stated by one and the same rule. Rule 90.1, for example, where Bae_2 eventually ends up always occurring after Bae_1, might mislead the reader in this respect because of the subscript numerals. The subscript numerals have not been used here in the sense of linearity; that is, Bae_1 means here 'one base' and Bae_2 means 'another base'. The subscript numeral symbols could be replaced by any better symbols, such as letters. Thus, Bae_1 could be written as Bae_m and Bae_2 as Bae_k, in order to avoid any linear interpretation. That is to say, Rule 90.1

has a selectional meaning only, namely that 'one base' is selected to be compounded with 'another base'. The fact that 90.1 is in essence selectional is evidenced by the addition of the linear rule 98. To make 98 operative Rule 97 is needed and to make Rule 97 operative Rule 90.1 is needed. Thus, from selection to linearity there is a chain-reaction in these rules.

Finally, the word order rules apply. All the concepts described above are now formed as words, defined by Rules 103–104.1. That is, we assume now that the following are the words formed by the application of the various rules mentioned above: *Ray, is, tiger-killer, a.* The word *is* is placed first (Rule 159), then *Ray* (160), and then *tiger-killer* (164). The article *a* is placed before its specified *tiger-killer* (Rule 180). Here too one may argue over whether rules like 178–180 should be applied before, say, rules like 159, 160, or 164. The point is whether such an ordering presents any conflict; we do not see any theoretical conflict in either ordering. However, what happens to the actual ordering in the psychological sense goes back once more to the problem of mental decisions (Chapter II).

Here we have seen that even a little sentence like (36i) needs the application of many rules. Other descriptive or generative models may use a much smaller number of rules, but in the long run, when more data is included, some of our same rules will apply to many other types of sentences or word formations. It is only then that we will observe a great degree of economy. Small chunks of data are likely to mislead the reader in viewing the economic aspect of our approach. The question, however, is not the number of rules, but rather whether all the necessary facts have been accounted for in the formation of a word or sentence. In a much wider sense total accountability, as Hockett (1947) would say, is the important consideration here.

BIBLIOGRAPHY

Baugh, Albert C. 1935. *A History of the English Language.* New York: Appleton-Century-Crofts.

Birdwhistell, R. 1970. *Kinesics and Context: Essays on Body Communicaton.* Philadelphia: University of Pennsylvania Press.

Bloch, B., and G.L. Trager. 1942. *Outline of Linguistic Analysis.* Baltimore: Linguistic Society of America.

Bloomfield, Leonard. 1933. *Language.* New York: Holt.

Carpenter, P.A., and M.A. Just. 1972. "Semantic Control of Eye Movements in Picture Scanning During a Sentence-picture Verification Task." *Perception and Psychophysics* 12:61-64

Chafe, Wallace L. 1970. *Meaning and the Structure of Language.* Chicago: University of Chicago Press.

———— 1971. "Directionality and Paraphrase." *Language* 47: 1-26

Chandola, Anoop. 1963. "Animal Commands of Garhwali and Their Linguistic Implications." *Word.* 19: 203-207.

———— 1966. *A Syntactic Sketch of Garhwali.* University of Chicago Ph.D. Dissertation in Linguistics. Ann Arbor: University Microfilms.

———— 1969. "Metalinguistic Structure of Indian Drumming: A Study in Musico-Linguistics." *Language and Style* 2: 288-295.

———— 1970. *A Systematic Translation of Hindi-Urdu into English.* Tucson: University of Arizona Press.

———— 1975. "An Evolutionary Approach to Sentence Formation." *Linguistics* 150: 15-46.

———— 1977. *Folk Drumming in the Himalayas: A Linguistic Approach to Music.* New York: AMS Press.

Chomsky, Noam. 1957. *Syntactic Structures.* The Hague: Mouton.

—— 1965. *Aspects of the Theory of Syntax.* Cambridge, Mass.: MIT Press.

Christie, William, Jr. (ed.) 1976. *Proceedings of the Second International Conference on Historical Linguistics.* Amsterdam: North-Holland Publishing Company.

Clark, Herbert H. 1965. "Some Structural Properties of Simple Active and Passive Sentences." *Journal of Verbal Learning and Verbal Behavior* 4: 365–370.

Coleman, E.B. 1965. "Learning of Prose Written in Four Grammatical Transformations." *Journal of Applied Psychology* 49: 332–341.

Fillmore, Charles J. 1968. "The Case for Case." *Universals in Linguistic theory,* ed. by Emmon Bach and Robert T. Harms. New York: Holt, 1–88.

Firbas, Jan. 1966 "Non-Thematic Subjects in Contemporary English." *Travaux Linguistiques de Prague* 2: 239–256.

Firth, J.R. 1957. *Papers in Linguistics, 1934–1951.* London: Oxford University Press.

Halle, Morris. 1962. "Phonology in Generative Grammar." *Word* 18: 54–72.

Halliday, M.A.K. 1967. "Notes on Transitivity and Theme in English, Part 2." *Journal of Linguistics* 3: 199–244.

Harris, Zellig. 1951. *Methods in Structural Linguistics.* Chicago: University of Chicago Press.

Hockett, Charles F. 1947. "Problems of Morphemic Analysis." *Language* 23: 321–343.

Iyer, K.A. Subramania. 1969. *Bhartṛhari: A Study of the Vākyapadīya in the Light of the Ancient Commentaries.* Poona: Deccan College.

Jackendoff, Ray. 1975. "Morphological and Semantic Regularities in the Lexicon." *Language* 51: 639–671.

Jakobson, Roman, C.G.M. Fant and M. Halle. 1963. *Preliminaries to Speech Analysis.* Cambridge, Mass.: MIT Press.

Jha, Ganganath. 1967. *The Kāvyaprakaśa of Mammaṭa.* Varanasi: Bharatiya Vidya Prakashan.

Johnson-Laird, P.N. 1968. "The Choice of the Passive Voice in a Communicative Task." *British Journal of Psychology* 59: 7–15.

Kintsch, W. 1974. *The Representation of Meaning in Memory.*

New York: Lawrence Erlbaum Associates.

Lamb, Sydney M. 1966. *Outline of Stratificational Grammar.* Washington, D.C.: Georgetown University Press.

Lehmann, W.P. 1974. *Proto-Indo-European Syntax.* Austin: University of Texas Press.

Lightner, Theodore M. 1975. "The Role of Derivational Morphology in Generative Grammar." *Language* 51: 617–638.

Lindsley, J.R. 1975. "Producing Simple Sentences: How Far Ahead Do We Plan?" *Cognitive Psychology* 7: 1–19.

MacWhinney, Brian. 1977. "Starting Points." *Language* 53: 152–168.

Martinet, A. 1962. *A Functional View of Language.* Oxford: Oxford University Press.

Morris, C.W. 1946. *Signs, Language and Behavior.* New York: Braziller.

Osgood, Charles. 1971 "Where Do Sentences Come From?" *Semantics*, ed. by D. Steinberg and L. Jakobovits. Cambridge: Cambridge University Press, 497–529.

Piaget, Jean. 1952. *The Origins of Intelligence in Children.* New York: International Universities Press.

—— ,and B. Inhelder. 1971. *Mental Imagery in the Child.* London: Routledge and Kegan Paul.

Pike, Kenneth L. 1947 *Phonemics: A Technique for Reducing Languages to Writing.* Ann Arbor: University of Michigan Press.

—— 1967. *Language in Relation to a Unified Theory of the Structure of Human Behavior.* 2d ed. The Hague: Mouton.

Prentice, Joan. 1966. "Response Strength of Single Words as an Influence in Sentence Behavior." *Journal of Verbal Learning and Verbal Behavior* 5: 429–433.

Raja, K. Kunjunni. 1963. *Indian Theories of Meaning.* Madras: The Adyar Library.

Sapir, Edward. 1921. *Language: An Introduction to the Study of Speech*: New York: Harcourt.

—— 1951. *Selected Writings of Edward Sapir in Language, Culture, and Personality.* Edited by David G. Mandelbaum. Berkeley and Los Angeles: University of California Press.

Saussure, Ferdinand de. 1959. *Course in General Linguistics.* Translated by Wade Baskin. New York: Philosophical Library.

Scheflen, Albert E. 1973. *Communicational Structure: Analysis of a Psychotherapy Transaction.* Bloomington: Indiana University Press.

Smith, John W. 1977. *The Behavior of Communicating: An Ethological Approach.* Cambridge, Massachusetts: Harvard University Press.

Sokolov, A.N. 1972. *Inner Speech and Thought.* New York: Plenum.

Staal, J. 1967. *Word Order in Sanskrit and Universal Grammar.* Dordrecht: Reidel.

Stevick, Robert D. 1968. *English and its History: The Evolution of a Language.* Boston: Allyn and Bacon.

Traugott, Elizabeth Closs. 1972. *A History of English Syntax.* New York: Holt, Rinehart and Winston.

Vasu, S.C. 1962. *Pāṇini: The Aṣṭādhyāyī.* Delhi: Motilal Banarasidass.

Wells, R.S. 1947. "Immediate Constituents." *Language* 23: 81–117.

Whorf, Benjamin Lee. 1965. *Language, Thought, and Reality: Selected Writings of Benjamin Lee Whorf.* Edited by John B. Carroll. Cambridge, Mass.: MIT Press.

Wright, Joseph. 1954. *Grammar of the Gothic Language.* 2d. ed. Oxford: Clarendon Press.